I0002754

GCC 7.0 GNU OpenMP

A catalogue record for this book is available from the Hong Kong Public Libraries.

Published in Hong Kong by Samurai Media Limited.

Email: info@samuraimedia.org

ISBN 978-988-8406-97-5

Background Cover Image by https://www.flickr.com/people/webtreatsetc/

Short Contents

Introduction 1
1 Enabling OpenMP 3
2 Runtime Library Routines 5
3 Environment Variables 19
4 Enabling OpenACC 25
5 OpenACC Runtime Library Routines 27
6 OpenACC Environment Variables 39
7 CUDA Streams Usage 41
8 OpenACC Library Interoperability 43
9 The libgomp ABI 47
10 Reporting Bugs 53
GNU General Public License 55
GNU Free Documentation License 67
Funding Free Software 75
Library Index 77

Table of Contents

Introduction 1

1 Enabling OpenMP 3

2 Runtime Library Routines 5

2.1 omp_get_active_level – Number of parallel regions 5
2.2 omp_get_ancestor_thread_num – Ancestor thread ID 5
2.3 omp_get_cancellation – Whether cancellation support is enabled 5
2.4 omp_get_default_device – Get the default device for target regions 6
2.5 omp_get_dynamic – Dynamic teams setting 6
2.6 omp_get_level – Obtain the current nesting level 6
2.7 omp_get_max_active_levels – Maximum number of active regions 7
2.8 omp_get_max_task_priority – Maximum priority value........ 7
2.9 omp_get_max_threads – Maximum number of threads of parallel region 7
2.10 omp_get_nested – Nested parallel regions 8
2.11 omp_get_num_devices – Number of target devices............. 8
2.12 omp_get_num_procs – Number of processors online 8
2.13 omp_get_num_teams – Number of teams 9
2.14 omp_get_num_threads – Size of the active team 9
2.15 omp_get_proc_bind – Whether theads may be moved between CPUs 9
2.16 omp_get_schedule – Obtain the runtime scheduling method .. 10
2.17 omp_get_team_num – Get team number 10
2.18 omp_get_team_size – Number of threads in a team 10
2.19 omp_get_thread_limit – Maximum number of threads 11
2.20 omp_get_thread_num – Current thread ID 11
2.21 omp_in_parallel – Whether a parallel region is active 11
2.22 omp_in_final – Whether in final or included task region 12
2.23 omp_is_initial_device – Whether executing on the host device 12
2.24 omp_set_default_device – Set the default device for target regions 12
2.25 omp_set_dynamic – Enable/disable dynamic teams 13
2.26 omp_set_max_active_levels – Limits the number of active parallel regions 13
2.27 omp_set_nested – Enable/disable nested parallel regions 13
2.28 omp_set_num_threads – Set upper team size limit 14
2.29 omp_set_schedule – Set the runtime scheduling method 14

2.30 omp_init_lock – Initialize simple lock 14
2.31 omp_set_lock – Wait for and set simple lock 15
2.32 omp_test_lock – Test and set simple lock if available 15
2.33 omp_unset_lock – Unset simple lock 15
2.34 omp_destroy_lock – Destroy simple lock 16
2.35 omp_init_nest_lock – Initialize nested lock 16
2.36 omp_set_nest_lock – Wait for and set nested lock 16
2.37 omp_test_nest_lock – Test and set nested lock if available .. 17
2.38 omp_unset_nest_lock – Unset nested lock 17
2.39 omp_destroy_nest_lock – Destroy nested lock 18
2.40 omp_get_wtick – Get timer precision 18
2.41 omp_get_wtime – Elapsed wall clock time 18

3 Environment Variables 19

3.1 OMP_CANCELLATION – Set whether cancellation is activated 19
3.2 OMP_DISPLAY_ENV – Show OpenMP version and environment variables 19
3.3 OMP_DEFAULT_DEVICE – Set the device used in target regions ... 19
3.4 OMP_DYNAMIC – Dynamic adjustment of threads 19
3.5 OMP_MAX_ACTIVE_LEVELS – Set the maximum number of nested parallel regions 20
3.6 OMP_MAX_TASK_PRIORITY – Set the maximum priority 20
3.7 OMP_NESTED – Nested parallel regions 20
3.8 OMP_NUM_THREADS – Specifies the number of threads to use 20
3.9 OMP_PROC_BIND – Whether theads may be moved between CPUs 20
3.10 OMP_PLACES – Specifies on which CPUs the theads should be placed 21
3.11 OMP_STACKSIZE – Set default thread stack size 22
3.12 OMP_SCHEDULE – How threads are scheduled 22
3.13 OMP_THREAD_LIMIT – Set the maximum number of threads 22
3.14 OMP_WAIT_POLICY – How waiting threads are handled 22
3.15 GOMP_CPU_AFFINITY – Bind threads to specific CPUs 23
3.16 GOMP_DEBUG – Enable debugging output 23
3.17 GOMP_STACKSIZE – Set default thread stack size 23
3.18 GOMP_SPINCOUNT – Set the busy-wait spin count 24
3.19 GOMP_RTEMS_THREAD_POOLS – Set the RTEMS specific thread pools 24

4 Enabling OpenACC 25

5 OpenACC Runtime Library Routines 27

5.1 acc_get_num_devices – Get number of devices for given device type 27
5.2 acc_set_device_type – Set type of device accelerator to use... 27
5.3 acc_get_device_type – Get type of device accelerator to be used. 27
5.4 acc_set_device_num – Set device number to use. 28
5.5 acc_get_device_num – Get device number to be used. 28
5.6 acc_async_test – Test for completion of a specific asynchronous operation. 28
5.7 acc_async_test_all – Tests for completion of all asynchronous operations. 29
5.8 acc_wait – Wait for completion of a specific asynchronous operation. 29
5.9 acc_wait_all – Waits for completion of all asynchronous operations. 29
5.10 acc_wait_all_async – Wait for completion of all asynchronous operations. 30
5.11 acc_wait_async – Wait for completion of asynchronous operations. 30
5.12 acc_init – Initialize runtime for a specific device type. 30
5.13 acc_shutdown – Shuts down the runtime for a specific device type. 30
5.14 acc_on_device – Whether executing on a particular device... 31
5.15 acc_malloc – Allocate device memory. 31
5.16 acc_free – Free device memory. 31
5.17 acc_copyin – Allocate device memory and copy host memory to it. 32
5.18 acc_present_or_copyin – If the data is not present on the device, allocate device memory and copy from host memory. 32
5.19 acc_create – Allocate device memory and map it to host memory. 33
5.20 acc_present_or_create – If the data is not present on the device, allocate device memory and map it to host memory. 33
5.21 acc_copyout – Copy device memory to host memory. 34
5.22 acc_delete – Free device memory. 34
5.23 acc_update_device – Update device memory from mapped host memory. 35
5.24 acc_update_self – Update host memory from mapped device memory. 35
5.25 acc_map_data – Map previously allocated device memory to host memory. 36
5.26 acc_unmap_data – Unmap device memory from host memory. 36
5.27 acc_deviceptr – Get device pointer associated with specific host address. 36
5.28 acc_hostptr – Get host pointer associated with specific device address. 36

5.29 `acc_is_present` – Indicate whether host variable / array is present on device 37
5.30 `acc_memcpy_to_device` – Copy host memory to device memory. 37
5.31 `acc_memcpy_from_device` – Copy device memory to host memory 37
5.32 `acc_get_current_cuda_device` – Get CUDA device handle. 38
5.33 `acc_get_current_cuda_context` – Get CUDA context handle. 38
5.34 `acc_get_cuda_stream` – Get CUDA stream handle 38
5.35 `acc_set_cuda_stream` – Set CUDA stream handle 38

6 OpenACC Environment Variables 39

6.1 `ACC_DEVICE_TYPE` 39
6.2 `ACC_DEVICE_NUM` 39
6.3 `GCC_ACC_NOTIFY` 39

7 CUDA Streams Usage 41

8 OpenACC Library Interoperability 43

8.1 Introduction 43
8.2 First invocation: NVIDIA CUBLAS library API 43
8.3 First invocation: OpenACC library API 44
8.4 OpenACC library and environment variables 45

9 The libgomp ABI 47

9.1 Implementing MASTER construct 47
9.2 Implementing CRITICAL construct 47
9.3 Implementing ATOMIC construct 47
9.4 Implementing FLUSH construct 47
9.5 Implementing BARRIER construct 47
9.6 Implementing THREADPRIVATE construct 47
9.7 Implementing PRIVATE clause 48
9.8 Implementing FIRSTPRIVATE LASTPRIVATE COPYIN and COPYPRIVATE clauses 48
9.9 Implementing REDUCTION clause 48
9.10 Implementing PARALLEL construct 48
9.11 Implementing FOR construct 49
9.12 Implementing ORDERED construct 50
9.13 Implementing SECTIONS construct 50
9.14 Implementing SINGLE construct 50
9.15 Implementing OpenACC's PARALLEL construct 51

10 Reporting Bugs 53

GNU General Public License 55

GNU Free Documentation License 67

ADDENDUM: How to use this License for your documents 74

Funding Free Software 75

Library Index 77

Introduction

This manual documents the usage of libgomp, the GNU Offloading and Multi Processing Runtime Library. This includes the GNU implementation of the OpenMP Application Programming Interface (API) for multi-platform shared-memory parallel programming in C/C++ and Fortran, and the GNU implementation of the OpenACC Application Programming Interface (API) for offloading of code to accelerator devices in C/C++ and Fortran.

Originally, libgomp implemented the GNU OpenMP Runtime Library. Based on this, support for OpenACC and offloading (both OpenACC and OpenMP 4's target construct) has been added later on, and the library's name changed to GNU Offloading and Multi Processing Runtime Library.

1 Enabling OpenMP

To activate the OpenMP extensions for C/C++ and Fortran, the compile-time flag `-fopenmp` must be specified. This enables the OpenMP directive `#pragma omp` in C/C++ and `!$omp` directives in free form, `c$omp`, `*$omp` and `!$omp` directives in fixed form, `!$` conditional compilation sentinels in free form and `c$`, `*$` and `!$` sentinels in fixed form, for Fortran. The flag also arranges for automatic linking of the OpenMP runtime library (Chapter 2 [Runtime Library Routines], page 5).

A complete description of all OpenMP directives accepted may be found in the OpenMP Application Program Interface manual, version 4.5.

2 Runtime Library Routines

The runtime routines described here are defined by Section 3 of the OpenMP specification in version 4.5. The routines are structured in following three parts:

2.1 `omp_get_active_level` – Number of parallel regions

Description:
This function returns the nesting level for the active parallel blocks, which enclose the calling call.

C/C++
Prototype: `int omp_get_active_level(void);`

Fortran:
Interface: `integer function omp_get_active_level()`

See also: Section 2.6 [omp_get_level], page 6, Section 2.7 [omp_get_max_active_levels], page 7, Section 2.26 [omp_set_max_active_levels], page 13

Reference: OpenMP specification v4.5, Section 3.2.20.

2.2 `omp_get_ancestor_thread_num` – Ancestor thread ID

Description:
This function returns the thread identification number for the given nesting level of the current thread. For values of *level* outside zero to `omp_get_level` -1 is returned; if *level* is `omp_get_level` the result is identical to `omp_get_thread_num`.

C/C++
Prototype: `int omp_get_ancestor_thread_num(int level);`

Fortran:
Interface:
```
integer function omp_get_ancestor_thread_num(level)
integer level
```

See also: Section 2.6 [omp_get_level], page 6, Section 2.20 [omp_get_thread_num], page 11, Section 2.18 [omp_get_team_size], page 10

Reference: OpenMP specification v4.5, Section 3.2.18.

2.3 `omp_get_cancellation` – Whether cancellation support is enabled

Description:
This function returns `true` if cancellation is activated, `false` otherwise. Here, `true` and `false` represent their language-specific counterparts. Unless `OMP_CANCELLATION` is set true, cancellations are deactivated.

C/C++:
Prototype: `int omp_get_cancellation(void);`

Fortran:

Interface: `logical function omp_get_cancellation()`

See also: Section 3.1 [OMP_CANCELLATION], page 19

Reference: OpenMP specification v4.5, Section 3.2.9.

2.4 omp_get_default_device – Get the default device for target regions

Description:

Get the default device for target regions without device clause.

C/C++:

Prototype: `int omp_get_default_device(void);`

Fortran:

Interface: `integer function omp_get_default_device()`

See also: Section 3.3 [OMP_DEFAULT_DEVICE], page 19, Section 2.24 [omp_set_default_device], page 12

Reference: OpenMP specification v4.5, Section 3.2.30.

2.5 omp_get_dynamic – Dynamic teams setting

Description:

This function returns `true` if enabled, `false` otherwise. Here, `true` and `false` represent their language-specific counterparts.

The dynamic team setting may be initialized at startup by the `OMP_DYNAMIC` environment variable or at runtime using `omp_set_dynamic`. If undefined, dynamic adjustment is disabled by default.

C/C++:

Prototype: `int omp_get_dynamic(void);`

Fortran:

Interface: `logical function omp_get_dynamic()`

See also: Section 2.25 [omp_set_dynamic], page 13, Section 3.4 [OMP_DYNAMIC], page 19

Reference: OpenMP specification v4.5, Section 3.2.8.

2.6 omp_get_level – Obtain the current nesting level

Description:

This function returns the nesting level for the parallel blocks, which enclose the calling call.

C/C++

Prototype: `int omp_get_level(void);`

Fortran:

Interface: `integer function omp_level()`

See also: Section 2.1 [omp_get_active_level], page 5

Reference: OpenMP specification v4.5, Section 3.2.17.

2.7 `omp_get_max_active_levels` – Maximum number of active regions

Description:
This function obtains the maximum allowed number of nested, active parallel regions.

C/C++

Prototype: `int omp_get_max_active_levels(void);`

Fortran:

Interface: `integer function omp_get_max_active_levels()`

See also: Section 2.26 [omp_set_max_active_levels], page 13, Section 2.1 [omp_get_active_level], page 5

Reference: OpenMP specification v4.5, Section 3.2.16.

2.8 `omp_get_max_task_priority` – Maximum priority value

that can be set for tasks.

Description:
This function obtains the maximum allowed priority number for tasks.

C/C++

Prototype: `int omp_get_max_task_priority(void);`

Fortran:

Interface: `integer function omp_get_max_task_priority()`

Reference: OpenMP specification v4.5, Section 3.2.29.

2.9 `omp_get_max_threads` – Maximum number of threads of parallel region

Description:
Return the maximum number of threads used for the current parallel region that does not use the clause `num_threads`.

C/C++:

Prototype: `int omp_get_max_threads(void);`

Fortran:

Interface: `integer function omp_get_max_threads()`

See also: Section 2.28 [omp_set_num_threads], page 14, Section 2.25 [omp_set_dynamic], page 13, Section 2.19 [omp_get_thread_limit], page 11

Reference: OpenMP specification v4.5, Section 3.2.3.

2.10 omp_get_nested – Nested parallel regions

Description:

This function returns **true** if nested parallel regions are enabled, **false** otherwise. Here, **true** and **false** represent their language-specific counterparts.

Nested parallel regions may be initialized at startup by the **OMP_NESTED** environment variable or at runtime using **omp_set_nested**. If undefined, nested parallel regions are disabled by default.

C/C++:

Prototype: `int omp_get_nested(void);`

Fortran:

Interface: `logical function omp_get_nested()`

See also: Section 2.27 [omp_set_nested], page 13, Section 3.7 [OMP_NESTED], page 20

Reference: OpenMP specification v4.5, Section 3.2.11.

2.11 omp_get_num_devices – Number of target devices

Description:

Returns the number of target devices.

C/C++:

Prototype: `int omp_get_num_devices(void);`

Fortran:

Interface: `integer function omp_get_num_devices()`

Reference: OpenMP specification v4.5, Section 3.2.31.

2.12 omp_get_num_procs – Number of processors online

Description:

Returns the number of processors online on that device.

C/C++:

Prototype: `int omp_get_num_procs(void);`

Fortran:

Interface: `integer function omp_get_num_procs()`

Reference: OpenMP specification v4.5, Section 3.2.5.

2.13 omp_get_num_teams – Number of teams

Description:
Returns the number of teams in the current team region.

C/C++:
Prototype: `int omp_get_num_teams(void);`

Fortran:
Interface: `integer function omp_get_num_teams()`

Reference: OpenMP specification v4.5, Section 3.2.32.

2.14 omp_get_num_threads – Size of the active team

Description:
Returns the number of threads in the current team. In a sequential section of the program `omp_get_num_threads` returns 1.

The default team size may be initialized at startup by the `OMP_NUM_THREADS` environment variable. At runtime, the size of the current team may be set either by the `NUM_THREADS` clause or by `omp_set_num_threads`. If none of the above were used to define a specific value and `OMP_DYNAMIC` is disabled, one thread per CPU online is used.

C/C++:
Prototype: `int omp_get_num_threads(void);`

Fortran:
Interface: `integer function omp_get_num_threads()`

See also: Section 2.9 [omp_get_max_threads], page 7, Section 2.28 [omp_set_num_threads], page 14, Section 3.8 [OMP_NUM_THREADS], page 20

Reference: OpenMP specification v4.5, Section 3.2.2.

2.15 omp_get_proc_bind – Whether theads may be moved between CPUs

Description:
This functions returns the currently active thread affinity policy, which is set via `OMP_PROC_BIND`. Possible values are `omp_proc_bind_false`, `omp_proc_bind_true`, `omp_proc_bind_master`, `omp_proc_bind_close` and `omp_proc_bind_spread`.

C/C++:
Prototype: `omp_proc_bind_t omp_get_proc_bind(void);`

Fortran:
Interface: `integer(kind=omp_proc_bind_kind) function omp_get_proc_bind()`

See also: Section 3.9 [OMP_PROC_BIND], page 20, Section 3.10 [OMP_PLACES], page 21, Section 3.15 [GOMP_CPU_AFFINITY], page 23,

Reference: OpenMP specification v4.5, Section 3.2.22.

2.16 `omp_get_schedule` – Obtain the runtime scheduling method

Description:

Obtain the runtime scheduling method. The *kind* argument will be set to the value `omp_sched_static`, `omp_sched_dynamic`, `omp_sched_guided` or `omp_sched_auto`. The second argument, *chunk_size*, is set to the chunk size.

C/C++

Prototype: `void omp_get_schedule(omp_sched_t *kind, int *chunk_size);`

Fortran:

Interface:

```
subroutine omp_get_schedule(kind, chunk_size)
integer(kind=omp_sched_kind) kind
integer chunk_size
```

See also: Section 2.29 [omp_set_schedule], page 14, Section 3.12 [OMP_SCHEDULE], page 22

Reference: OpenMP specification v4.5, Section 3.2.13.

2.17 `omp_get_team_num` – Get team number

Description:

Returns the team number of the calling thread.

C/C++:

Prototype: `int omp_get_team_num(void);`

Fortran:

Interface: `integer function omp_get_team_num()`

Reference: OpenMP specification v4.5, Section 3.2.33.

2.18 `omp_get_team_size` – Number of threads in a team

Description:

This function returns the number of threads in a thread team to which either the current thread or its ancestor belongs. For values of *level* outside zero to `omp_get_level`, -1 is returned; if *level* is zero, 1 is returned, and for `omp_get_level`, the result is identical to `omp_get_num_threads`.

C/C++:

Prototype: `int omp_get_team_size(int level);`

Fortran:

Interface:

```
integer function omp_get_team_size(level)
integer level
```

See also: Section 2.14 [omp_get_num_threads], page 9, Section 2.6 [omp_get_level], page 6, Section 2.2 [omp_get_ancestor_thread_num], page 5

Reference: OpenMP specification v4.5, Section 3.2.19.

2.19 `omp_get_thread_limit` – Maximum number of threads

Description:
Return the maximum number of threads of the program.

C/C++:
Prototype: `int omp_get_thread_limit(void);`

Fortran:
Interface: `integer function omp_get_thread_limit()`

See also: Section 2.9 [omp_get_max_threads], page 7, Section 3.13 [OMP_THREAD_LIMIT], page 22

Reference: OpenMP specification v4.5, Section 3.2.14.

2.20 `omp_get_thread_num` – Current thread ID

Description:
Returns a unique thread identification number within the current team. In a sequential parts of the program, `omp_get_thread_num` always returns 0. In parallel regions the return value varies from 0 to `omp_get_num_threads`-1 inclusive. The return value of the master thread of a team is always 0.

C/C++:
Prototype: `int omp_get_thread_num(void);`

Fortran:
Interface: `integer function omp_get_thread_num()`

See also: Section 2.14 [omp_get_num_threads], page 9, Section 2.2 [omp_get_ancestor_thread_num], page 5

Reference: OpenMP specification v4.5, Section 3.2.4.

2.21 `omp_in_parallel` – Whether a parallel region is active

Description:
This function returns `true` if currently running in parallel, `false` otherwise. Here, `true` and `false` represent their language-specific counterparts.

C/C++:
Prototype: `int omp_in_parallel(void);`

Fortran:
Interface: `logical function omp_in_parallel()`

Reference: OpenMP specification v4.5, Section 3.2.6.

2.22 omp_in_final – Whether in final or included task region

Description:
This function returns true if currently running in a final or included task region, false otherwise. Here, true and false represent their language-specific counterparts.

C/C++:
Prototype: `int omp_in_final(void);`

Fortran:
Interface: `logical function omp_in_final()`

Reference: OpenMP specification v4.5, Section 3.2.21.

2.23 omp_is_initial_device – Whether executing on the host device

Description:
This function returns true if currently running on the host device, false otherwise. Here, true and false represent their language-specific counterparts.

C/C++:
Prototype: `int omp_is_initial_device(void);`

Fortran:
Interface: `logical function omp_is_initial_device()`

Reference: OpenMP specification v4.5, Section 3.2.34.

2.24 omp_set_default_device – Set the default device for target regions

Description:
Set the default device for target regions without device clause. The argument shall be a nonnegative device number.

C/C++:
Prototype: `void omp_set_default_device(int device_num);`

Fortran:
Interface:
```
subroutine omp_set_default_device(device_num)
integer device_num
```

See also: Section 3.3 [OMP_DEFAULT_DEVICE], page 19, Section 2.4 [omp_get_default_device], page 6

Reference: OpenMP specification v4.5, Section 3.2.29.

2.25 `omp_set_dynamic` – Enable/disable dynamic teams

Description:

Enable or disable the dynamic adjustment of the number of threads within a team. The function takes the language-specific equivalent of `true` and `false`, where `true` enables dynamic adjustment of team sizes and `false` disables it.

C/C++:

Prototype: `void omp_set_dynamic(int dynamic_threads);`

Fortran:

Interface:
```
subroutine omp_set_dynamic(dynamic_threads)
logical, intent(in) :: dynamic_threads
```

See also: Section 3.4 [OMP_DYNAMIC], page 19, Section 2.5 [omp_get_dynamic], page 6

Reference: OpenMP specification v4.5, Section 3.2.7.

2.26 `omp_set_max_active_levels` – Limits the number of active parallel regions

Description:

This function limits the maximum allowed number of nested, active parallel regions.

C/C++

Prototype: `void omp_set_max_active_levels(int max_levels);`

Fortran:

Interface:
```
subroutine omp_set_max_active_levels(max_levels)
integer max_levels
```

See also: Section 2.7 [omp_get_max_active_levels], page 7, Section 2.1 [omp_get_active_level], page 5

Reference: OpenMP specification v4.5, Section 3.2.15.

2.27 `omp_set_nested` – Enable/disable nested parallel regions

Description:

Enable or disable nested parallel regions, i.e., whether team members are allowed to create new teams. The function takes the language-specific equivalent of `true` and `false`, where `true` enables dynamic adjustment of team sizes and `false` disables it.

C/C++:

Prototype: `void omp_set_nested(int nested);`

Fortran:

Interface:
```
subroutine omp_set_nested(nested)
logical, intent(in) :: nested
```

See also: Section 3.7 [OMP_NESTED], page 20, Section 2.10 [omp_get_nested], page 8

Reference: OpenMP specification v4.5, Section 3.2.10.

2.28 omp_set_num_threads – Set upper team size limit

Description:
Specifies the number of threads used by default in subsequent parallel sections, if those do not specify a **num_threads** clause. The argument of **omp_set_num_threads** shall be a positive integer.

C/C++:
Prototype: `void omp_set_num_threads(int num_threads);`

Fortran:
Interface:
```
subroutine omp_set_num_threads(num_threads)
integer, intent(in) :: num_threads
```

See also: Section 3.8 [OMP_NUM_THREADS], page 20, Section 2.14 [omp_get_num_threads], page 9, Section 2.9 [omp_get_max_threads], page 7

Reference: OpenMP specification v4.5, Section 3.2.1.

2.29 omp_set_schedule – Set the runtime scheduling method

Description:
Sets the runtime scheduling method. The *kind* argument can have the value **omp_sched_static**, **omp_sched_dynamic**, **omp_sched_guided** or **omp_sched_auto**. Except for **omp_sched_auto**, the chunk size is set to the value of *chunk_size* if positive, or to the default value if zero or negative. For **omp_sched_auto** the *chunk_size* argument is ignored.

C/C++
Prototype: `void omp_set_schedule(omp_sched_t kind, int chunk_size);`

Fortran:
Interface:
```
subroutine omp_set_schedule(kind, chunk_size)
integer(kind=omp_sched_kind) kind
integer chunk_size
```

See also: Section 2.16 [omp_get_schedule], page 10 Section 3.12 [OMP_SCHEDULE], page 22

Reference: OpenMP specification v4.5, Section 3.2.12.

2.30 omp_init_lock – Initialize simple lock

Description:
Initialize a simple lock. After initialization, the lock is in an unlocked state.

C/C++:
Prototype: `void omp_init_lock(omp_lock_t *lock);`

Fortran:
Interface:
```
subroutine omp_init_lock(svar)
integer(omp_lock_kind), intent(out) :: svar
```

See also: Section 2.34 [omp_destroy_lock], page 16

Reference: OpenMP specification v4.5, Section 3.3.1.

2.31 `omp_set_lock` – Wait for and set simple lock

Description:

Before setting a simple lock, the lock variable must be initialized by `omp_init_lock`. The calling thread is blocked until the lock is available. If the lock is already held by the current thread, a deadlock occurs.

C/C++:

Prototype: `void omp_set_lock(omp_lock_t *lock);`

Fortran:

Interface:
```
subroutine omp_set_lock(svar)
integer(omp_lock_kind), intent(inout) :: svar
```

See also: Section 2.30 [omp_init_lock], page 14, Section 2.32 [omp_test_lock], page 15, Section 2.33 [omp_unset_lock], page 15

Reference: OpenMP specification v4.5, Section 3.3.4.

2.32 `omp_test_lock` – Test and set simple lock if available

Description:

Before setting a simple lock, the lock variable must be initialized by `omp_init_lock`. Contrary to `omp_set_lock`, `omp_test_lock` does not block if the lock is not available. This function returns `true` upon success, `false` otherwise. Here, `true` and `false` represent their language-specific counterparts.

C/C++:

Prototype: `int omp_test_lock(omp_lock_t *lock);`

Fortran:

Interface:
```
logical function omp_test_lock(svar)
integer(omp_lock_kind), intent(inout) :: svar
```

See also: Section 2.30 [omp_init_lock], page 14, Section 2.31 [omp_set_lock], page 15, Section 2.31 [omp_set_lock], page 15

Reference: OpenMP specification v4.5, Section 3.3.6.

2.33 `omp_unset_lock` – Unset simple lock

Description:

A simple lock about to be unset must have been locked by `omp_set_lock` or `omp_test_lock` before. In addition, the lock must be held by the thread calling `omp_unset_lock`. Then, the lock becomes unlocked. If one or more threads attempted to set the lock before, one of them is chosen to, again, set the lock to itself.

C/C++:

Prototype: `void omp_unset_lock(omp_lock_t *lock);`

Fortran:

Interface:
```
subroutine omp_unset_lock(svar)
integer(omp_lock_kind), intent(inout) :: svar
```

See also: Section 2.31 [omp_set_lock], page 15, Section 2.32 [omp_test_lock], page 15

Reference: OpenMP specification v4.5, Section 3.3.5.

2.34 `omp_destroy_lock` – Destroy simple lock

Description:

Destroy a simple lock. In order to be destroyed, a simple lock must be in the unlocked state.

C/C++:

Prototype: `void omp_destroy_lock(omp_lock_t *lock);`

Fortran:

Interface:
```
subroutine omp_destroy_lock(svar)
integer(omp_lock_kind), intent(inout) :: svar
```

See also: Section 2.30 [omp_init_lock], page 14

Reference: OpenMP specification v4.5, Section 3.3.3.

2.35 `omp_init_nest_lock` – Initialize nested lock

Description:

Initialize a nested lock. After initialization, the lock is in an unlocked state and the nesting count is set to zero.

C/C++:

Prototype: `void omp_init_nest_lock(omp_nest_lock_t *lock);`

Fortran:

Interface:
```
subroutine omp_init_nest_lock(nvar)
integer(omp_nest_lock_kind), intent(out) :: nvar
```

See also: Section 2.39 [omp_destroy_nest_lock], page 18

Reference: OpenMP specification v4.5, Section 3.3.1.

2.36 `omp_set_nest_lock` – Wait for and set nested lock

Description:

Before setting a nested lock, the lock variable must be initialized by `omp_init_nest_lock`. The calling thread is blocked until the lock is available. If the lock is already held by the current thread, the nesting count for the lock is incremented.

C/C++:

Prototype: `void omp_set_nest_lock(omp_nest_lock_t *lock);`

Fortran:

Interface:
```
subroutine omp_set_nest_lock(nvar)
integer(omp_nest_lock_kind), intent(inout) :: nvar
```

See also: Section 2.35 [omp_init_nest_lock], page 16, Section 2.38 [omp_unset_nest_lock], page 17

Reference: OpenMP specification v4.5, Section 3.3.4.

2.37 omp_test_nest_lock – Test and set nested lock if available

Description:

Before setting a nested lock, the lock variable must be initialized by `omp_init_nest_lock`. Contrary to `omp_set_nest_lock`, `omp_test_nest_lock` does not block if the lock is not available. If the lock is already held by the current thread, the new nesting count is returned. Otherwise, the return value equals zero.

C/C++:

Prototype: `int omp_test_nest_lock(omp_nest_lock_t *lock);`

Fortran:

Interface:
```
logical function omp_test_nest_lock(nvar)
integer(omp_nest_lock_kind), intent(inout) :: nvar
```

See also: Section 2.30 [omp_init_lock], page 14, Section 2.31 [omp_set_lock], page 15, Section 2.31 [omp_set_lock], page 15

Reference: OpenMP specification v4.5, Section 3.3.6.

2.38 omp_unset_nest_lock – Unset nested lock

Description:

A nested lock about to be unset must have been locked by `omp_set_nested_lock` or `omp_test_nested_lock` before. In addition, the lock must be held by the thread calling `omp_unset_nested_lock`. If the nesting count drops to zero, the lock becomes unlocked. If one ore more threads attempted to set the lock before, one of them is chosen to, again, set the lock to itself.

C/C++:

Prototype: `void omp_unset_nest_lock(omp_nest_lock_t *lock);`

Fortran:

Interface:
```
subroutine omp_unset_nest_lock(nvar)
integer(omp_nest_lock_kind), intent(inout) :: nvar
```

See also: Section 2.36 [omp_set_nest_lock], page 16

Reference: OpenMP specification v4.5, Section 3.3.5.

2.39 `omp_destroy_nest_lock` – Destroy nested lock

Description:
Destroy a nested lock. In order to be destroyed, a nested lock must be in the unlocked state and its nesting count must equal zero.

C/C++:
Prototype: `void omp_destroy_nest_lock(omp_nest_lock_t *);`

Fortran:
Interface:
```
subroutine omp_destroy_nest_lock(nvar)
integer(omp_nest_lock_kind), intent(inout) :: nvar
```

See also: Section 2.30 [omp_init_lock], page 14

Reference: OpenMP specification v4.5, Section 3.3.3.

2.40 `omp_get_wtick` – Get timer precision

Description:
Gets the timer precision, i.e., the number of seconds between two successive clock ticks.

C/C++:
Prototype: `double omp_get_wtick(void);`

Fortran:
Interface: `double precision function omp_get_wtick()`

See also: Section 2.41 [omp_get_wtime], page 18

Reference: OpenMP specification v4.5, Section 3.4.2.

2.41 `omp_get_wtime` – Elapsed wall clock time

Description:
Elapsed wall clock time in seconds. The time is measured per thread, no guarantee can be made that two distinct threads measure the same time. Time is measured from some "time in the past", which is an arbitrary time guaranteed not to change during the execution of the program.

C/C++:
Prototype: `double omp_get_wtime(void);`

Fortran:
Interface: `double precision function omp_get_wtime()`

See also: Section 2.40 [omp_get_wtick], page 18

Reference: OpenMP specification v4.5, Section 3.4.1.

3 Environment Variables

The environment variables which beginning with `OMP_` are defined by section 4 of the OpenMP specification in version 4.5, while those beginning with `GOMP_` are GNU extensions.

3.1 OMP_CANCELLATION – Set whether cancellation is activated

Description:
If set to `TRUE`, the cancellation is activated. If set to `FALSE` or if unset, cancellation is disabled and the `cancel` construct is ignored.

See also: Section 2.3 [omp_get_cancellation], page 5

Reference: OpenMP specification v4.5, Section 4.11

3.2 OMP_DISPLAY_ENV – Show OpenMP version and environment variables

Description:
If set to `TRUE`, the OpenMP version number and the values associated with the OpenMP environment variables are printed to `stderr`. If set to `VERBOSE`, it additionally shows the value of the environment variables which are GNU extensions. If undefined or set to `FALSE`, this information will not be shown.

Reference: OpenMP specification v4.5, Section 4.12

3.3 OMP_DEFAULT_DEVICE – Set the device used in target regions

Description:
Set to choose the device which is used in a `target` region, unless the value is overridden by `omp_set_default_device` or by a `device` clause. The value shall be the nonnegative device number. If no device with the given device number exists, the code is executed on the host. If unset, device number 0 will be used.

See also: Section 2.4 [omp_get_default_device], page 6, Section 2.24 [omp_set_default_device], page 12,

Reference: OpenMP specification v4.5, Section 4.13

3.4 OMP_DYNAMIC – Dynamic adjustment of threads

Description:
Enable or disable the dynamic adjustment of the number of threads within a team. The value of this environment variable shall be `TRUE` or `FALSE`. If undefined, dynamic adjustment is disabled by default.

See also: Section 2.25 [omp_set_dynamic], page 13

Reference: OpenMP specification v4.5, Section 4.3

3.5 OMP_MAX_ACTIVE_LEVELS – Set the maximum number of nested parallel regions

Description:

Specifies the initial value for the maximum number of nested parallel regions. The value of this variable shall be a positive integer. If undefined, the number of active levels is unlimited.

See also: Section 2.26 [omp_set_max_active_levels], page 13

Reference: OpenMP specification v4.5, Section 4.9

3.6 OMP_MAX_TASK_PRIORITY – Set the maximum priority

number that can be set for a task.

Description:

Specifies the initial value for the maximum priority value that can be set for a task. The value of this variable shall be a non-negative integer, and zero is allowed. If undefined, the default priority is 0.

See also: Section 2.8 [omp_get_max_task_priority], page 7

Reference: OpenMP specification v4.5, Section 4.14

3.7 OMP_NESTED – Nested parallel regions

Description:

Enable or disable nested parallel regions, i.e., whether team members are allowed to create new teams. The value of this environment variable shall be `TRUE` or `FALSE`. If undefined, nested parallel regions are disabled by default.

See also: Section 2.27 [omp_set_nested], page 13

Reference: OpenMP specification v4.5, Section 4.6

3.8 OMP_NUM_THREADS – Specifies the number of threads to use

Description:

Specifies the default number of threads to use in parallel regions. The value of this variable shall be a comma-separated list of positive integers; the value specified the number of threads to use for the corresponding nested level. If undefined one thread per CPU is used.

See also: Section 2.28 [omp_set_num_threads], page 14

Reference: OpenMP specification v4.5, Section 4.2

3.9 OMP_PROC_BIND – Whether theads may be moved between CPUs

Description:

Specifies whether threads may be moved between processors. If set to `TRUE`, OpenMP theads should not be moved; if set to `FALSE` they may be moved. Alternatively, a comma separated list with the values `MASTER`, `CLOSE` and `SPREAD` can be used to specify the thread affinity policy for the corresponding nesting level. With MASTER the worker threads are in the same place partition as the master thread. With CLOSE those are kept close to the master thread in contiguous place partitions. And with SPREAD a sparse distribution across the place partitions is used.

When undefined, OMP_PROC_BIND defaults to TRUE when OMP_PLACES or GOMP_CPU_AFFINITY is set and FALSE otherwise.

See also: Section 3.10 [OMP_PLACES], page 21, Section 3.15 [GOMP_CPU_AFFINITY], page 23, Section 2.15 [omp_get_proc_bind], page 9

Reference: OpenMP specification v4.5, Section 4.4

3.10 OMP_PLACES – Specifies on which CPUs the theads should be placed

Description:

The thread placement can be either specified using an abstract name or by an explicit list of the places. The abstract names threads, cores and sockets can be optionally followed by a positive number in parentheses, which denotes the how many places shall be created. With threads each place corresponds to a single hardware thread; cores to a single core with the corresponding number of hardware threads; and with sockets the place corresponds to a single socket. The resulting placement can be shown by setting the OMP_DISPLAY_ENV environment variable.

Alternatively, the placement can be specified explicitly as comma-separated list of places. A place is specified by set of nonnegative numbers in curly braces, denoting the denoting the hardware threads. The hardware threads belonging to a place can either be specified as comma-separated list of nonnegative thread numbers or using an interval. Multiple places can also be either specified by a comma-separated list of places or by an interval. To specify an interval, a colon followed by the count is placed after after the hardware thread number or the place. Optionally, the length can be followed by a colon and the stride number – otherwise a unit stride is assumed. For instance, the following specifies the same places list: "{0,1,2}, {3,4,6}, {7,8,9}, {10,11,12}"; "{0:3}, {3:3}, {7:3}, {10:3}"; and "{0:2}:4:3".

If OMP_PLACES and GOMP_CPU_AFFINITY are unset and OMP_PROC_BIND is either unset or false, threads may be moved between CPUs following no placement policy.

See also: Section 3.9 [OMP_PROC_BIND], page 20, Section 3.15 [GOMP_CPU_AFFINITY], page 23, Section 2.15 [omp_get_proc_bind], page 9, Section 3.2 [OMP_DISPLAY_ENV], page 19

Reference: OpenMP specification v4.5, Section 4.5

3.11 OMP_STACKSIZE – Set default thread stack size

Description:
Set the default thread stack size in kilobytes, unless the number is suffixed by B, K, M or G, in which case the size is, respectively, in bytes, kilobytes, megabytes or gigabytes. This is different from pthread_attr_setstacksize which gets the number of bytes as an argument. If the stack size cannot be set due to system constraints, an error is reported and the initial stack size is left unchanged. If undefined, the stack size is system dependent.

Reference: OpenMP specification v4.5, Section 4.7

3.12 OMP_SCHEDULE – How threads are scheduled

Description:
Allows to specify **schedule type** and **chunk size**. The value of the variable shall have the form: type[,chunk] where type is one of static, dynamic, guided or auto The optional chunk size shall be a positive integer. If undefined, dynamic scheduling and a chunk size of 1 is used.

See also: Section 2.29 [omp_set_schedule], page 14

Reference: OpenMP specification v4.5, Sections 2.7.1.1 and 4.1

3.13 OMP_THREAD_LIMIT – Set the maximum number of threads

Description:
Specifies the number of threads to use for the whole program. The value of this variable shall be a positive integer. If undefined, the number of threads is not limited.

See also: Section 3.8 [OMP_NUM_THREADS], page 20, Section 2.19 [omp_get_thread_limit], page 11

Reference: OpenMP specification v4.5, Section 4.10

3.14 OMP_WAIT_POLICY – How waiting threads are handled

Description:
Specifies whether waiting threads should be active or passive. If the value is PASSIVE, waiting threads should not consume CPU power while waiting; while the value is ACTIVE specifies that they should. If undefined, threads wait actively for a short time before waiting passively.

See also: Section 3.18 [GOMP_SPINCOUNT], page 24

Reference: OpenMP specification v4.5, Section 4.8

3.15 GOMP_CPU_AFFINITY – Bind threads to specific CPUs

Description:

Binds threads to specific CPUs. The variable should contain a space-separated or comma-separated list of CPUs. This list may contain different kinds of entries: either single CPU numbers in any order, a range of CPUs (M-N) or a range with some stride (M-N:S). CPU numbers are zero based. For example, `GOMP_CPU_AFFINITY="0 3 1-2 4-15:2"` will bind the initial thread to CPU 0, the second to CPU 3, the third to CPU 1, the fourth to CPU 2, the fifth to CPU 4, the sixth through tenth to CPUs 6, 8, 10, 12, and 14 respectively and then start assigning back from the beginning of the list. `GOMP_CPU_AFFINITY=0` binds all threads to CPU 0.

There is no libgomp library routine to determine whether a CPU affinity specification is in effect. As a workaround, language-specific library functions, e.g., `getenv` in C or `GET_ENVIRONMENT_VARIABLE` in Fortran, may be used to query the setting of the `GOMP_CPU_AFFINITY` environment variable. A defined CPU affinity on startup cannot be changed or disabled during the runtime of the application.

If both `GOMP_CPU_AFFINITY` and `OMP_PROC_BIND` are set, `OMP_PROC_BIND` has a higher precedence. If neither has been set and `OMP_PROC_BIND` is unset, or when `OMP_PROC_BIND` is set to `FALSE`, the host system will handle the assignment of threads to CPUs.

See also: Section 3.10 [OMP_PLACES], page 21, Section 3.9 [OMP_PROC_BIND], page 20

3.16 GOMP_DEBUG – Enable debugging output

Description:

Enable debugging output. The variable should be set to `0` (disabled, also the default if not set), or `1` (enabled).

If enabled, some debugging output will be printed during execution. This is currently not specified in more detail, and subject to change.

3.17 GOMP_STACKSIZE – Set default thread stack size

Description:

Set the default thread stack size in kilobytes. This is different from `pthread_attr_setstacksize` which gets the number of bytes as an argument. If the stack size cannot be set due to system constraints, an error is reported and the initial stack size is left unchanged. If undefined, the stack size is system dependent.

See also: Section 3.11 [OMP_STACKSIZE], page 22

Reference: GCC Patches Mailinglist, GCC Patches Mailinglist

3.18 GOMP_SPINCOUNT – Set the busy-wait spin count

Description:

Determines how long a threads waits actively with consuming CPU power before waiting passively without consuming CPU power. The value may be either INFINITE, INFINITY to always wait actively or an integer which gives the number of spins of the busy-wait loop. The integer may optionally be followed by the following suffixes acting as multiplication factors: k (kilo, thousand), M (mega, million), G (giga, billion), or T (tera, trillion). If undefined, 0 is used when OMP_WAIT_POLICY is PASSIVE, 300,000 is used when OMP_WAIT_POLICY is undefined and 30 billion is used when OMP_WAIT_POLICY is ACTIVE. If there are more OpenMP threads than available CPUs, 1000 and 100 spins are used for OMP_WAIT_POLICY being ACTIVE or undefined, respectively; unless the GOMP_SPINCOUNT is lower or OMP_WAIT_POLICY is PASSIVE.

See also: Section 3.14 [OMP_WAIT_POLICY], page 22

3.19 GOMP_RTEMS_THREAD_POOLS – Set the RTEMS specific thread pools

Description:

This environment variable is only used on the RTEMS real-time operating system. It determines the scheduler instance specific thread pools. The format for GOMP_RTEMS_THREAD_POOLS is a list of optional <thread-pool-count>[$<priority>]@<scheduler-name> configurations separated by : where:

- <thread-pool-count> is the thread pool count for this scheduler instance.
- $<priority> is an optional priority for the worker threads of a thread pool according to pthread_setschedparam. In case a priority value is omitted, then a worker thread will inherit the priority of the OpenMP master thread that created it. The priority of the worker thread is not changed after creation, even if a new OpenMP master thread using the worker has a different priority.
- @<scheduler-name> is the scheduler instance name according to the RTEMS application configuration.

In case no thread pool configuration is specified for a scheduler instance, then each OpenMP master thread of this scheduler instance will use its own dynamically allocated thread pool. To limit the worker thread count of the thread pools, each OpenMP master thread must call omp_set_num_threads.

Example: Lets suppose we have three scheduler instances IO, WRK0, and WRK1 with GOMP_RTEMS_THREAD_POOLS set to "1@WRK0:3$4@WRK1". Then there are no thread pool restrictions for scheduler instance IO. In the scheduler instance WRK0 there is one thread pool available. Since no priority is specified for this scheduler instance, the worker thread inherits the priority of the OpenMP master thread that created it. In the scheduler instance WRK1 there are three thread pools available and their worker threads run at priority four.

4 Enabling OpenACC

To activate the OpenACC extensions for C/C++ and Fortran, the compile-time flag '-fopenacc' must be specified. This enables the OpenACC directive #pragma acc in C/C++ and !$accp directives in free form, c$acc, *$acc and !$acc directives in fixed form, !$ conditional compilation sentinels in free form and c$, *$ and !$ sentinels in fixed form, for Fortran. The flag also arranges for automatic linking of the OpenACC runtime library (Chapter 5 [OpenACC Runtime Library Routines], page 27).

A complete description of all OpenACC directives accepted may be found in the OpenACC Application Programming Interface manual, version 2.0.

Note that this is an experimental feature and subject to change in future versions of GCC. See https://gcc.gnu.org/wiki/OpenACC for more information.

5 OpenACC Runtime Library Routines

The runtime routines described here are defined by section 3 of the OpenACC specifications in version 2.0. They have C linkage, and do not throw exceptions. Generally, they are available only for the host, with the exception of `acc_on_device`, which is available for both the host and the acceleration device.

5.1 `acc_get_num_devices` – Get number of devices for given device type

Description

This function returns a value indicating the number of devices available for the device type specified in *devicetype*.

C/C++:

Prototype: `int acc_get_num_devices(acc_device_t devicetype);`

Fortran:

Interface:

```
integer function acc_get_num_devices(devicetype)
integer(kind=acc_device_kind) devicetype
```

Reference: OpenACC specification v2.0, section 3.2.1.

5.2 `acc_set_device_type` – Set type of device accelerator to use.

Description

This function indicates to the runtime library which device typr, specified in *devicetype*, to use when executing a parallel or kernels region.

C/C++:

Prototype: `acc_set_device_type(acc_device_t devicetype);`

Fortran:

Interface:

```
subroutine acc_set_device_type(devicetype)
integer(kind=acc_device_kind) devicetype
```

Reference: OpenACC specification v2.0, section 3.2.2.

5.3 `acc_get_device_type` – Get type of device accelerator to be used.

Description

This function returns what device type will be used when executing a parallel or kernels region.

C/C++:

Prototype: `acc_device_t acc_get_device_type(void);`

Fortran:

Interface:

```
function acc_get_device_type(void)
integer(kind=acc_device_kind) acc_get_device_type
```

Reference: OpenACC specification v2.0, section 3.2.3.

5.4 acc_set_device_num – Set device number to use.

Description

This function will indicate to the runtime which device number, specified by *num*, associated with the specifed device type *devicetype*.

C/C++:

Prototype: `acc_set_device_num(int num, acc_device_t devicetype);`

Fortran:

Interface:
```
subroutine acc_set_device_num(devicenum, devicetype)
integer devicenum
integer(kind=acc_device_kind) devicetype
```

Reference: OpenACC specification v2.0, section 3.2.4.

5.5 acc_get_device_num – Get device number to be used.

Description

This function returns which device number associated with the specified device type *devicetype*, will be used when executing a parallel or kernels region.

C/C++:

Prototype: `int acc_get_device_num(acc_device_t devicetype);`

Fortran:

Interface:
```
function acc_get_device_num(devicetype)
integer(kind=acc_device_kind) devicetype
integer acc_get_device_num
```

Reference: OpenACC specification v2.0, section 3.2.5.

5.6 acc_async_test – Test for completion of a specific asynchronous operation.

Description

This function tests for completion of the asynchrounous operation specified in *arg*. In C/C++, a non-zero value will be returned to indicate the specified asynchronous operation has completed. While Fortran will return a `true`. If the asynchrounous operation has not completed, C/C++ returns a zero and Fortran returns a `false`.

C/C++:

Prototype: `int acc_async_test(int arg);`

Fortran:

Interface:
```
function acc_async_test(arg)
integer(kind=acc_handle_kind) arg
logical acc_async_test
```

Reference: OpenACC specification v2.0, section 3.2.6.

5.7 acc_async_test_all – Tests for completion of all asynchronous operations.

Description

This function tests for completion of all asynchrounous operations. In C/C++, a non-zero value will be returned to indicate all asynchronous operations have completed. While Fortran will return a `true`. If any asynchronous operation has not completed, C/C++ returns a zero and Fortran returns a `false`.

C/C++:

Prototype: `int acc_async_test_all(void);`

Fortran:

Interface: `function acc_async_test()`
`logical acc_get_device_num`

Reference: OpenACC specification v2.0, section 3.2.7.

5.8 acc_wait – Wait for completion of a specific asynchronous operation.

Description

This function waits for completion of the asynchronous operation specified in *arg*.

C/C++:

Prototype: `acc_wait(arg);`

Fortran:

Interface: `subroutine acc_wait(arg)`
`integer(acc_handle_kind) arg`

Reference: OpenACC specification v2.0, section 3.2.8.

5.9 acc_wait_all – Waits for completion of all asynchronous operations.

Description

This function waits for the completion of all asynchronous operations.

C/C++:

Prototype: `acc_wait_all(void);`

Fortran:

Interface: `subroutine acc_wait_async()`

Reference: OpenACC specification v2.0, section 3.2.10.

5.10 `acc_wait_all_async` – Wait for completion of all asynchronous operations.

Description

This function enqueues a wait operation on the queue *async* for any and all asynchronous operations that have been previously enqueued on any queue.

C/C++:

Prototype: `acc_wait_all_async(int async);`

Fortran:

Interface:
```
subroutine acc_wait_all_async(async)
integer(acc_handle_kind) async
```

Reference: OpenACC specification v2.0, section 3.2.11.

5.11 `acc_wait_async` – Wait for completion of asynchronous operations.

Description

This function enqueues a wait operation on queue *async* for any and all asynchronous operations enqueued on queue *arg*.

C/C++:

Prototype: `acc_wait_async(int arg, int async);`

Fortran:

Interface:
```
subroutine acc_wait_async(arg, async)
integer(acc_handle_kind) arg, async
```

Reference: OpenACC specification v2.0, section 3.2.9.

5.12 `acc_init` – Initialize runtime for a specific device type.

Description

This function initializes the runtime for the device type specified in *devicetype*.

C/C++:

Prototype: `acc_init(acc_device_t devicetype);`

Fortran:

Interface:
```
subroutine acc_init(devicetype)
integer(acc_device_kind) devicetype
```

Reference: OpenACC specification v2.0, section 3.2.12.

5.13 `acc_shutdown` – Shuts down the runtime for a specific device type.

Description

This function shuts down the runtime for the device type specified in *devicetype*.

C/C++:

Prototype: `acc_shutdown(acc_device_t devicetype);`

Fortran:

Interface:
```
subroutine acc_shutdown(devicetype)
integer(acc_device_kind) devicetype
```

Reference: OpenACC specification v2.0, section 3.2.13.

5.14 acc_on_device – Whether executing on a particular device

Description:

This function returns whether the program is executing on a particular device specified in *devicetype*. In C/C++ a non-zero value is returned to indicate the device is execiting on the specified device type. In Fortran, `true` will be returned. If the program is not executing on the specified device type C/C++ will return a zero, while Fortran will return `false`.

C/C++:

Prototype: `acc_on_device(acc_device_t devicetype);`

Fortran:

Interface:
```
function acc_on_device(devicetype)
integer(acc_device_kind) devicetype
logical acc_on_device
```

Reference: OpenACC specification v2.0, section 3.2.14.

5.15 acc_malloc – Allocate device memory.

Description

This function allocates *len* bytes of device memory. It returns the device address of the allocated memory.

C/C++:

Prototype: `d_void* acc_malloc(size_t len);`

Reference: OpenACC specification v2.0, section 3.2.15.

5.16 acc_free – Free device memory.

Description

Free previously allocated device memory at the device address `a`.

C/C++:

Prototype: `acc_free(d_void *a);`

Reference: OpenACC specification v2.0, section 3.2.16.

5.17 acc_copyin – Allocate device memory and copy host memory to it.

Description

In C/C++, this function allocates *len* bytes of device memory and maps it to the specified host address in *a*. The device address of the newly allocated device memory is returned.

In Fortran, two (2) forms are supported. In the first form, *a* specifies a contiguous array section. The second form *a* specifies a variable or array element and *len* specifies the length in bytes.

C/C++:

Prototype: `void *acc_copyin(h_void *a, size_t len);`

Fortran:

Interface:
```
subroutine acc_copyin(a)
type, dimension(:[,:]...) :: a
```
Interface:
```
subroutine acc_copyin(a, len)
type, dimension(:[,:]...) :: a
integer len
```

Reference: OpenACC specification v2.0, section 3.2.17.

5.18 acc_present_or_copyin – If the data is not present on the device, allocate device memory and copy from host memory.

Description

This function tests if the host data specifed by *a* and of length *len* is present or not. If it is not present, then device memory will be allocated and the host memory copied. The device address of the newly allocated device memory is returned.

In Fortran, two (2) forms are supported. In the first form, *a* specifies a contiguous array section. The second form *a* specifies a variable or array element and *len* specifies the length in bytes.

C/C++:

Prototype: `void *acc_present_or_copyin(h_void *a, size_t len);`

Prototype: `void *acc_pcopyin(h_void *a, size_t len);`

Fortran:

Interface:
```
subroutine acc_present_or_copyin(a)
type, dimension(:[,:]...) :: a
```
Interface:
```
subroutine acc_present_or_copyin(a, len)
type, dimension(:[,:]...) :: a
integer len
```
Interface:
```
subroutine acc_pcopyin(a)
type, dimension(:[,:]...) :: a
```
Interface:
```
subroutine acc_pcopyin(a, len)
type, dimension(:[,:]...) :: a
```

```
integer len
```

Reference: OpenACC specification v2.0, section 3.2.18.

5.19 acc_create – Allocate device memory and map it to host memory.

Description

This function allocates device memory and maps it to host memory specified by the host address *a* with a length of *len* bytes. In C/C++, the function returns the device address of the allocated device memory.

In Fortran, two (2) forms are supported. In the first form, *a* specifies a contiguous array section. The second form *a* specifies a variable or array element and *len* specifies the length in bytes.

C/C++:

Prototype: `void *acc_create(h_void *a, size_t len);`

Fortran:

Interface:
```
subroutine acc_create(a)
type, dimension(:[,:]...) :: a
```
Interface:
```
subroutine acc_create(a, len)
type, dimension(:[,:]...) :: a
integer len
```

Reference: OpenACC specification v2.0, section 3.2.19.

5.20 acc_present_or_create – If the data is not present on the device, allocate device memory and map it to host memory.

Description

This function tests if the host data specifed by *a* and of length *len* is present or not. If it is not present, then device memory will be allocated and mapped to host memory. In C/C++, the device address of the newly allocated device memory is returned.

In Fortran, two (2) forms are supported. In the first form, *a* specifies a contiguous array section. The second form *a* specifies a variable or array element and *len* specifies the length in bytes.

C/C++:

Prototype: `void *acc_present_or_create(h_void *a, size_t len)`
Prototype: `void *acc_pcreate(h_void *a, size_t len)`

Fortran:

Interface:
```
subroutine acc_present_or_create(a)
type, dimension(:[,:]...) :: a
```
Interface:
```
subroutine acc_present_or_create(a, len)
type, dimension(:[,:]...) :: a
```

	`integer len`
Interface:	`subroutine acc_pcreate(a)`
	`type, dimension(:[,:]...) :: a`
Interface:	`subroutine acc_pcreate(a, len)`
	`type, dimension(:[,:]...) :: a`
	`integer len`

Reference: OpenACC specification v2.0, section 3.2.20.

5.21 acc_copyout – Copy device memory to host memory.

Description

This function copies mapped device memory to host memory which is specified by host address *a* for a length *len* bytes in C/C++.

In Fortran, two (2) forms are supported. In the first form, *a* specifies a contiguous array section. The second form *a* specifies a variable or array element and *len* specifies the length in bytes.

C/C++:

Prototype: `acc_copyout(h_void *a, size_t len);`

Fortran:

Interface:	`subroutine acc_copyout(a)`
	`type, dimension(:[,:]...) :: a`
Interface:	`subroutine acc_copyout(a, len)`
	`type, dimension(:[,:]...) :: a`
	`integer len`

Reference: OpenACC specification v2.0, section 3.2.21.

5.22 acc_delete – Free device memory.

Description

This function frees previously allocated device memory specified by the device address *a* and the length of *len* bytes.

In Fortran, two (2) forms are supported. In the first form, *a* specifies a contiguous array section. The second form *a* specifies a variable or array element and *len* specifies the length in bytes.

C/C++:

Prototype: `acc_delete(h_void *a, size_t len);`

Fortran:

Interface:	`subroutine acc_delete(a)`
	`type, dimension(:[,:]...) :: a`
Interface:	`subroutine acc_delete(a, len)`
	`type, dimension(:[,:]...) :: a`
	`integer len`

Reference: OpenACC specification v2.0, section 3.2.22.

5.23 acc_update_device – Update device memory from mapped host memory.

Description

This function updates the device copy from the previously mapped host memory. The host memory is specified with the host address *a* and a length of *len* bytes.

In Fortran, two (2) forms are supported. In the first form, *a* specifies a contiguous array section. The second form *a* specifies a variable or array element and *len* specifies the length in bytes.

C/C++:

Prototype: `acc_update_device(h_void *a, size_t len);`

Fortran:

Interface:
```
subroutine acc_update_device(a)
type, dimension(:[,:]...) :: a
```
Interface:
```
subroutine acc_update_device(a, len)
type, dimension(:[,:]...) :: a
integer len
```

Reference: OpenACC specification v2.0, section 3.2.23.

5.24 acc_update_self – Update host memory from mapped device memory.

Description

This function updates the host copy from the previously mapped device memory. The host memory is specified with the host address *a* and a length of *len* bytes.

In Fortran, two (2) forms are supported. In the first form, *a* specifies a contiguous array section. The second form *a* specifies a variable or array element and *len* specifies the length in bytes.

C/C++:

Prototype: `acc_update_self(h_void *a, size_t len);`

Fortran:

Interface:
```
subroutine acc_update_self(a)
type, dimension(:[,:]...) :: a
```
Interface:
```
subroutine acc_update_self(a, len)
type, dimension(:[,:]...) :: a
integer len
```

Reference: OpenACC specification v2.0, section 3.2.24.

5.25 `acc_map_data` – Map previously allocated device memory to host memory.

Description

This function maps previously allocated device and host memory. The device memory is specified with the device address *d*. The host memory is specified with the host address *h* and a length of *len*.

C/C++:

Prototype: `acc_map_data(h_void *h, d_void *d, size_t len);`

Reference: OpenACC specification v2.0, section 3.2.25.

5.26 `acc_unmap_data` – Unmap device memory from host memory.

Description

This function unmaps previously mapped device and host memory. The latter specified by *h*.

C/C++:

Prototype: `acc_unmap_data(h_void *h);`

Reference: OpenACC specification v2.0, section 3.2.26.

5.27 `acc_deviceptr` – Get device pointer associated with specific host address.

Description

This function returns the device address that has been mapped to the host address specified by *h*.

C/C++:

Prototype: `void *acc_deviceptr(h_void *h);`

Reference: OpenACC specification v2.0, section 3.2.27.

5.28 `acc_hostptr` – Get host pointer associated with specific device address.

Description

This function returns the host address that has been mapped to the device address specified by *d*.

C/C++:

Prototype: `void *acc_hostptr(d_void *d);`

Reference: OpenACC specification v2.0, section 3.2.28.

5.29 acc_is_present – Indicate whether host variable / array is present on device.

Description

This function indicates whether the specified host address in *a* and a length of *len* bytes is present on the device. In C/C++, a non-zero value is returned to indicate the presence of the mapped memory on the device. A zero is returned to indicate the memory is not mapped on the device.

In Fortran, two (2) forms are supported. In the first form, *a* specifies a contiguous array section. The second form *a* specifies a variable or array element and *len* specifies the length in bytes. If the host memory is mapped to device memory, then a `true` is returned. Otherwise, a `false` is return to indicate the mapped memory is not present.

C/C++:

Prototype:
```
int acc_is_present(h_void *a, size_t len);
```

Fortran:

Interface:
```
function acc_is_present(a)
type, dimension(:[,:]...) :: a
logical acc_is_present
```

Interface:
```
function acc_is_present(a, len)
type, dimension(:[,:]...) :: a
integer len
logical acc_is_present
```

Reference: OpenACC specification v2.0, section 3.2.29.

5.30 acc_memcpy_to_device – Copy host memory to device memory.

Description

This function copies host memory specified by host address of *src* to device memory specified by the device address *dest* for a length of *bytes* bytes.

C/C++:

Prototype:
```
acc_memcpy_to_device(d_void *dest, h_void *src, size_t
bytes);
```

Reference: OpenACC specification v2.0, section 3.2.30.

5.31 acc_memcpy_from_device – Copy device memory to host memory.

Description

This function copies host memory specified by host address of *src* from device memory specified by the device address *dest* for a length of *bytes* bytes.

C/C++:

Prototype:
```
acc_memcpy_from_device(d_void *dest, h_void *src, size_t
bytes);
```

Reference: OpenACC specification v2.0, section 3.2.31.

5.32 acc_get_current_cuda_device – Get CUDA device handle.

Description
This function returns the CUDA device handle. This handle is the same as used by the CUDA Runtime or Driver API's.

C/C++:
Prototype: `void *acc_get_current_cuda_device(void);`

Reference: OpenACC specification v2.0, section A.2.1.1.

5.33 acc_get_current_cuda_context – Get CUDA context handle.

Description
This function returns the CUDA context handle. This handle is the same as used by the CUDA Runtime or Driver API's.

C/C++:
Prototype: `acc_get_current_cuda_context(void);`

Reference: OpenACC specification v2.0, section A.2.1.2.

5.34 acc_get_cuda_stream – Get CUDA stream handle.

Description
This function returns the CUDA stream handle. This handle is the same as used by the CUDA Runtime or Driver API's.

C/C++:
Prototype: `acc_get_cuda_stream(void);`

Reference: OpenACC specification v2.0, section A.2.1.3.

5.35 acc_set_cuda_stream – Set CUDA stream handle.

Description
This function associates the stream handle specified by *stream* with the asynchronous value specified by *async*.

C/C++:
Prototype: `acc_set_cuda_stream(int async void *stream);`

Reference: OpenACC specification v2.0, section A.2.1.4.

6 OpenACC Environment Variables

The variables `ACC_DEVICE_TYPE` and `ACC_DEVICE_NUM` are defined by section 4 of the OpenACC specification in version 2.0. The variable `GCC_ACC_NOTIFY` is used for diagnostic purposes.

6.1 ACC_DEVICE_TYPE

Reference: OpenACC specification v2.0, section 4.1.

6.2 ACC_DEVICE_NUM

Reference: OpenACC specification v2.0, section 4.2.

6.3 GCC_ACC_NOTIFY

Description:

Print debug information pertaining to the accelerator.

7 CUDA Streams Usage

This applies to the `nvptx` plugin only.

The library provides elements that perform asynchronous movement of data and asynchronous operation of computing constructs. This asynchronous functionality is implemented by making use of CUDA streams[1].

The primary means by that the asychronous functionality is accessed is through the use of those OpenACC directives which make use of the `async` and `wait` clauses. When the `async` clause is first used with a directive, it creates a CUDA stream. If an `async-argument` is used with the `async` clause, then the stream is associated with the specified `async-argument`.

Following the creation of an association between a CUDA stream and the `async-argument` of an `async` clause, both the `wait` clause and the `wait` directive can be used. When either the clause or directive is used after stream creation, it creates a rendezvous point whereby execution waits until all operations associated with the `async-argument`, that is, stream, have completed.

Normally, the management of the streams that are created as a result of using the `async` clause, is done without any intervention by the caller. This implies the association between the `async-argument` and the CUDA stream will be maintained for the lifetime of the program. However, this association can be changed through the use of the library function `acc_set_cuda_stream`. When the function `acc_set_cuda_stream` is called, the CUDA stream that was originally associated with the `async` clause will be destroyed. Caution should be taken when changing the association as subsequent references to the `async-argument` refer to a different CUDA stream.

---

[1] See "Stream Management" in "CUDA Driver API", TRM-06703-001, Version 5.5, for additional information

8 OpenACC Library Interoperability

8.1 Introduction

The OpenACC library uses the CUDA Driver API, and may interact with programs that use the Runtime library directly, or another library based on the Runtime library, e.g., CUBLAS[1]. This chapter describes the use cases and what changes are required in order to use both the OpenACC library and the CUBLAS and Runtime libraries within a program.

8.2 First invocation: NVIDIA CUBLAS library API

In this first use case (see below), a function in the CUBLAS library is called prior to any of the functions in the OpenACC library. More specifically, the function `cublasCreate()`.

When invoked, the function initializes the library and allocates the hardware resources on the host and the device on behalf of the caller. Once the initialization and allocation has completed, a handle is returned to the caller. The OpenACC library also requires initialization and allocation of hardware resources. Since the CUBLAS library has already allocated the hardware resources for the device, all that is left to do is to initialize the OpenACC library and acquire the hardware resources on the host.

Prior to calling the OpenACC function that initializes the library and allocate the host hardware resources, you need to acquire the device number that was allocated during the call to `cublasCreate()`. The invoking of the runtime library function `cudaGetDevice()` accomplishes this. Once acquired, the device number is passed along with the device type as parameters to the OpenACC library function `acc_set_device_num()`.

Once the call to `acc_set_device_num()` has completed, the OpenACC library uses the context that was created during the call to `cublasCreate()`. In other words, both libraries will be sharing the same context.

```
/* Create the handle */
s = cublasCreate(&h);
if (s != CUBLAS_STATUS_SUCCESS)
{
    fprintf(stderr, "cublasCreate failed %d\n", s);
    exit(EXIT_FAILURE);
}

/* Get the device number */
e = cudaGetDevice(&dev);
if (e != cudaSuccess)
{
    fprintf(stderr, "cudaGetDevice failed %d\n", e);
    exit(EXIT_FAILURE);
}

/* Initialize OpenACC library and use device 'dev' */
acc_set_device_num(dev, acc_device_nvidia);
```

Use Case 1

[1] See section 2.26, "Interactions with the CUDA Driver API" in "CUDA Runtime API", Version 5.5, and section 2.27, "VDPAU Interoperability", in "CUDA Driver API", TRM-06703-001, Version 5.5, for additional information on library interoperability.

8.3 First invocation: OpenACC library API

In this second use case (see below), a function in the OpenACC library is called prior to any of the functions in the CUBLAS library. More specificially, the function `acc_set_device_num()`.

In the use case presented here, the function `acc_set_device_num()` is used to both initialize the OpenACC library and allocate the hardware resources on the host and the device. In the call to the function, the call parameters specify which device to use and what device type to use, i.e., `acc_device_nvidia`. It should be noted that this is but one method to initialize the OpenACC library and allocate the appropriate hardware resources. Other methods are available through the use of environment variables and these will be discussed in the next section.

Once the call to `acc_set_device_num()` has completed, other OpenACC functions can be called as seen with multiple calls being made to `acc_copyin()`. In addition, calls can be made to functions in the CUBLAS library. In the use case a call to `cublasCreate()` is made subsequent to the calls to `acc_copyin()`. As seen in the previous use case, a call to `cublasCreate()` initializes the CUBLAS library and allocates the hardware resources on the host and the device. However, since the device has already been allocated, `cublasCreate()` will only initialize the CUBLAS library and allocate the appropriate hardware resources on the host. The context that was created as part of the OpenACC initialization is shared with the CUBLAS library, similarly to the first use case.

```
dev = 0;

acc_set_device_num(dev, acc_device_nvidia);

/* Copy the first set to the device */
d_X = acc_copyin(&h_X[0], N * sizeof (float));
if (d_X == NULL)
{
    fprintf(stderr, "copyin error h_X\n");
    exit(EXIT_FAILURE);
}

/* Copy the second set to the device */
d_Y = acc_copyin(&h_Y1[0], N * sizeof (float));
if (d_Y == NULL)
{
    fprintf(stderr, "copyin error h_Y1\n");
    exit(EXIT_FAILURE);
}

/* Create the handle */
s = cublasCreate(&h);
if (s != CUBLAS_STATUS_SUCCESS)
{
    fprintf(stderr, "cublasCreate failed %d\n", s);
    exit(EXIT_FAILURE);
}

/* Perform saxpy using CUBLAS library function */
s = cublasSaxpy(h, N, &alpha, d_X, 1, d_Y, 1);
if (s != CUBLAS_STATUS_SUCCESS)
{
```

```
        fprintf(stderr, "cublasSaxpy failed %d\n", s);
        exit(EXIT_FAILURE);
    }

    /* Copy the results from the device */
    acc_memcpy_from_device(&h_Y1[0], d_Y, N * sizeof (float));
```

Use Case 2

8.4 OpenACC library and environment variables

There are two environment variables associated with the OpenACC library that may be used to control the device type and device number: `ACC_DEVICE_TYPE` and `ACC_DEVICE_NUM`, respecively. These two environement variables can be used as an alternative to calling `acc_set_device_num()`. As seen in the second use case, the device type and device number were specified using `acc_set_device_num()`. If however, the aforementioned environment variables were set, then the call to `acc_set_device_num()` would not be required.

The use of the environment variables is only relevant when an OpenACC function is called prior to a call to `cudaCreate()`. If `cudaCreate()` is called prior to a call to an OpenACC function, then you must call `acc_set_device_num()`[2]

---

[2] More complete information about `ACC_DEVICE_TYPE` and `ACC_DEVICE_NUM` can be found in sections 4.1 and 4.2 of the OpenACC Application Programming Interface, Version 2.0.

9 The libgomp ABI

The following sections present notes on the external ABI as presented by libgomp. Only maintainers should need them.

9.1 Implementing MASTER construct

```
if (omp_get_thread_num () == 0)
  block
```

Alternately, we generate two copies of the parallel subfunction and only include this in the version run by the master thread. Surely this is not worthwhile though...

9.2 Implementing CRITICAL construct

Without a specified name,

```
void GOMP_critical_start (void);
void GOMP_critical_end (void);
```

so that we don't get COPY relocations from libgomp to the main application.

With a specified name, use omp_set_lock and omp_unset_lock with name being transformed into a variable declared like

```
omp_lock_t gomp_critical_user_<name> __attribute__((common))
```

Ideally the ABI would specify that all zero is a valid unlocked state, and so we wouldn't need to initialize this at startup.

9.3 Implementing ATOMIC construct

The target should implement the `__sync` builtins.

Failing that we could add

```
void GOMP_atomic_enter (void)
void GOMP_atomic_exit (void)
```

which reuses the regular lock code, but with yet another lock object private to the library.

9.4 Implementing FLUSH construct

Expands to the `__sync_synchronize` builtin.

9.5 Implementing BARRIER construct

```
void GOMP_barrier (void)
```

9.6 Implementing THREADPRIVATE construct

In _most_ cases we can map this directly to `__thread`. Except that OMP allows constructors for C++ objects. We can either refuse to support this (how often is it used?) or we can implement something akin to .ctors.

Even more ideally, this ctor feature is handled by extensions to the main pthreads library. Failing that, we can have a set of entry points to register ctor functions to be called.

9.7 Implementing PRIVATE clause

In association with a PARALLEL, or within the lexical extent of a PARALLEL block, the variable becomes a local variable in the parallel subfunction.

In association with FOR or SECTIONS blocks, create a new automatic variable within the current function. This preserves the semantic of new variable creation.

9.8 Implementing FIRSTPRIVATE LASTPRIVATE COPYIN and COPYPRIVATE clauses

This seems simple enough for PARALLEL blocks. Create a private struct for communicating between the parent and subfunction. In the parent, copy in values for scalar and "small" structs; copy in addresses for others TREE_ADDRESSABLE types. In the subfunction, copy the value into the local variable.

It is not clear what to do with bare FOR or SECTION blocks. The only thing I can figure is that we do something like:

```
#pragma omp for firstprivate(x) lastprivate(y)
for (int i = 0; i < n; ++i)
  body;
```

which becomes

```
{
  int x = x, y;

  // for stuff

  if (i == n)
    y = y;
}
```

where the "x=x" and "y=y" assignments actually have different uids for the two variables, i.e. not something you could write directly in C. Presumably this only makes sense if the "outer" x and y are global variables.

COPYPRIVATE would work the same way, except the structure broadcast would have to happen via SINGLE machinery instead.

9.9 Implementing REDUCTION clause

The private struct mentioned in the previous section should have a pointer to an array of the type of the variable, indexed by the thread's *team_id*. The thread stores its final value into the array, and after the barrier, the master thread iterates over the array to collect the values.

9.10 Implementing PARALLEL construct

```
#pragma omp parallel
{
  body;
}
```

becomes

```
void subfunction (void *data)
{
```

```
    use data;
    body;
  }

  setup data;
  GOMP_parallel_start (subfunction, &data, num_threads);
  subfunction (&data);
  GOMP_parallel_end ();
```

```
void GOMP_parallel_start (void (*fn)(void *), void *data, unsigned num_threads)
```

The *FN* argument is the subfunction to be run in parallel.

The *DATA* argument is a pointer to a structure used to communicate data in and out of the subfunction, as discussed above with respect to FIRSTPRIVATE et al.

The *NUM_THREADS* argument is 1 if an IF clause is present and false, or the value of the NUM_THREADS clause, if present, or 0.

The function needs to create the appropriate number of threads and/or launch them from the dock. It needs to create the team structure and assign team ids.

```
void GOMP_parallel_end (void)
```

Tears down the team and returns us to the previous `omp_in_parallel()` state.

9.11 Implementing FOR construct

```
  #pragma omp parallel for
  for (i = lb; i <= ub; i++)
    body;
```

becomes

```
  void subfunction (void *data)
  {
    long _s0, _e0;
    while (GOMP_loop_static_next (&_s0, &_e0))
    {
      long _e1 = _e0, i;
      for (i = _s0; i < _e1; i++)
        body;
    }
    GOMP_loop_end_nowait ();
  }

  GOMP_parallel_loop_static (subfunction, NULL, 0, lb, ub+1, 1, 0);
  subfunction (NULL);
  GOMP_parallel_end ();
```

```
  #pragma omp for schedule(runtime)
  for (i = 0; i < n; i++)
    body;
```

becomes

```
  {
    long i, _s0, _e0;
    if (GOMP_loop_runtime_start (0, n, 1, &_s0, &_e0))
      do {
        long _e1 = _e0;
        for (i = _s0, i < _e0; i++)
          body;
      } while (GOMP_loop_runtime_next (&_s0, _&e0));
```

```
  GOMP_loop_end ();
}
```

Note that while it looks like there is trickiness to propagating a non-constant STEP, there isn't really. We're explicitly allowed to evaluate it as many times as we want, and any variables involved should automatically be handled as PRIVATE or SHARED like any other variables. So the expression should remain evaluable in the subfunction. We can also pull it into a local variable if we like, but since its supposed to remain unchanged, we can also not if we like.

If we have SCHEDULE(STATIC), and no ORDERED, then we ought to be able to get away with no work-sharing context at all, since we can simply perform the arithmetic directly in each thread to divide up the iterations. Which would mean that we wouldn't need to call any of these routines.

There are separate routines for handling loops with an ORDERED clause. Bookkeeping for that is non-trivial...

9.12 Implementing ORDERED construct

```
void GOMP_ordered_start (void)
void GOMP_ordered_end (void)
```

9.13 Implementing SECTIONS construct

A block as

```
#pragma omp sections
{
  #pragma omp section
  stmt1;
  #pragma omp section
  stmt2;
  #pragma omp section
  stmt3;
}
```

becomes

```
for (i = GOMP_sections_start (3); i != 0; i = GOMP_sections_next ())
  switch (i)
    {
    case 1:
      stmt1;
      break;
    case 2:
      stmt2;
      break;
    case 3:
      stmt3;
      break;
    }
GOMP_barrier ();
```

9.14 Implementing SINGLE construct

A block like

```
#pragma omp single
{
  body;
}
```

becomes

```
if (GOMP_single_start ())
  body;
GOMP_barrier ();
```

while

```
#pragma omp single copyprivate(x)
  body;
```

becomes

```
datap = GOMP_single_copy_start ();
if (datap == NULL)
  {
    body;
    data.x = x;
    GOMP_single_copy_end (&data);
  }
else
  x = datap->x;
GOMP_barrier ();
```

9.15 Implementing OpenACC's PARALLEL construct

```
void GOACC_parallel ()
```

10 Reporting Bugs

Bugs in the GNU Offloading and Multi Processing Runtime Library should be reported via Bugzilla. Please add "openacc", or "openmp", or both to the keywords field in the bug report, as appropriate.

GNU General Public License

Version 3, 29 June 2007

Preamble

The GNU General Public License is a free, copyleft license for software and other kinds of works.

The licenses for most software and other practical works are designed to take away your freedom to share and change the works. By contrast, the GNU General Public License is intended to guarantee your freedom to share and change all versions of a program–to make sure it remains free software for all its users. We, the Free Software Foundation, use the GNU General Public License for most of our software; it applies also to any other work released this way by its authors. You can apply it to your programs, too.

When we speak of free software, we are referring to freedom, not price. Our General Public Licenses are designed to make sure that you have the freedom to distribute copies of free software (and charge for them if you wish), that you receive source code or can get it if you want it, that you can change the software or use pieces of it in new free programs, and that you know you can do these things.

To protect your rights, we need to prevent others from denying you these rights or asking you to surrender the rights. Therefore, you have certain responsibilities if you distribute copies of the software, or if you modify it: responsibilities to respect the freedom of others.

For example, if you distribute copies of such a program, whether gratis or for a fee, you must pass on to the recipients the same freedoms that you received. You must make sure that they, too, receive or can get the source code. And you must show them these terms so they know their rights.

Developers that use the GNU GPL protect your rights with two steps: (1) assert copyright on the software, and (2) offer you this License giving you legal permission to copy, distribute and/or modify it.

For the developers' and authors' protection, the GPL clearly explains that there is no warranty for this free software. For both users' and authors' sake, the GPL requires that modified versions be marked as changed, so that their problems will not be attributed erroneously to authors of previous versions.

Some devices are designed to deny users access to install or run modified versions of the software inside them, although the manufacturer can do so. This is fundamentally incompatible with the aim of protecting users' freedom to change the software. The systematic pattern of such abuse occurs in the area of products for individuals to use, which is precisely where it is most unacceptable. Therefore, we have designed this version of the GPL to prohibit the practice for those products. If such problems arise substantially in other domains, we stand ready to extend this provision to those domains in future versions of the GPL, as needed to protect the freedom of users.

Finally, every program is threatened constantly by software patents. States should not allow patents to restrict development and use of software on general-purpose computers, but in those that do, we wish to avoid the special danger that patents applied to a free program could make it effectively proprietary. To prevent this, the GPL assures that patents cannot be used to render the program non-free.

The precise terms and conditions for copying, distribution and modification follow.

TERMS AND CONDITIONS

0. Definitions.

   "This License" refers to version 3 of the GNU General Public License.

   "Copyright" also means copyright-like laws that apply to other kinds of works, such as semiconductor masks.

   "The Program" refers to any copyrightable work licensed under this License. Each licensee is addressed as "you". "Licensees" and "recipients" may be individuals or organizations.

   To "modify" a work means to copy from or adapt all or part of the work in a fashion requiring copyright permission, other than the making of an exact copy. The resulting work is called a "modified version" of the earlier work or a work "based on" the earlier work.

   A "covered work" means either the unmodified Program or a work based on the Program.

   To "propagate" a work means to do anything with it that, without permission, would make you directly or secondarily liable for infringement under applicable copyright law, except executing it on a computer or modifying a private copy. Propagation includes copying, distribution (with or without modification), making available to the public, and in some countries other activities as well.

   To "convey" a work means any kind of propagation that enables other parties to make or receive copies. Mere interaction with a user through a computer network, with no transfer of a copy, is not conveying.

   An interactive user interface displays "Appropriate Legal Notices" to the extent that it includes a convenient and prominently visible feature that (1) displays an appropriate copyright notice, and (2) tells the user that there is no warranty for the work (except to the extent that warranties are provided), that licensees may convey the work under this License, and how to view a copy of this License. If the interface presents a list of user commands or options, such as a menu, a prominent item in the list meets this criterion.

1. Source Code.

   The "source code" for a work means the preferred form of the work for making modifications to it. "Object code" means any non-source form of a work.

   A "Standard Interface" means an interface that either is an official standard defined by a recognized standards body, or, in the case of interfaces specified for a particular programming language, one that is widely used among developers working in that language.

The "System Libraries" of an executable work include anything, other than the work as a whole, that (a) is included in the normal form of packaging a Major Component, but which is not part of that Major Component, and (b) serves only to enable use of the work with that Major Component, or to implement a Standard Interface for which an implementation is available to the public in source code form. A "Major Component", in this context, means a major essential component (kernel, window system, and so on) of the specific operating system (if any) on which the executable work runs, or a compiler used to produce the work, or an object code interpreter used to run it.

The "Corresponding Source" for a work in object code form means all the source code needed to generate, install, and (for an executable work) run the object code and to modify the work, including scripts to control those activities. However, it does not include the work's System Libraries, or general-purpose tools or generally available free programs which are used unmodified in performing those activities but which are not part of the work. For example, Corresponding Source includes interface definition files associated with source files for the work, and the source code for shared libraries and dynamically linked subprograms that the work is specifically designed to require, such as by intimate data communication or control flow between those subprograms and other parts of the work.

The Corresponding Source need not include anything that users can regenerate automatically from other parts of the Corresponding Source.

The Corresponding Source for a work in source code form is that same work.

2. Basic Permissions.

   All rights granted under this License are granted for the term of copyright on the Program, and are irrevocable provided the stated conditions are met. This License explicitly affirms your unlimited permission to run the unmodified Program. The output from running a covered work is covered by this License only if the output, given its content, constitutes a covered work. This License acknowledges your rights of fair use or other equivalent, as provided by copyright law.

   You may make, run and propagate covered works that you do not convey, without conditions so long as your license otherwise remains in force. You may convey covered works to others for the sole purpose of having them make modifications exclusively for you, or provide you with facilities for running those works, provided that you comply with the terms of this License in conveying all material for which you do not control copyright. Those thus making or running the covered works for you must do so exclusively on your behalf, under your direction and control, on terms that prohibit them from making any copies of your copyrighted material outside their relationship with you.

   Conveying under any other circumstances is permitted solely under the conditions stated below. Sublicensing is not allowed; section 10 makes it unnecessary.

3. Protecting Users' Legal Rights From Anti-Circumvention Law.

   No covered work shall be deemed part of an effective technological measure under any applicable law fulfilling obligations under article 11 of the WIPO copyright treaty adopted on 20 December 1996, or similar laws prohibiting or restricting circumvention of such measures.

When you convey a covered work, you waive any legal power to forbid circumvention of technological measures to the extent such circumvention is effected by exercising rights under this License with respect to the covered work, and you disclaim any intention to limit operation or modification of the work as a means of enforcing, against the work's users, your or third parties' legal rights to forbid circumvention of technological measures.

4. Conveying Verbatim Copies.

   You may convey verbatim copies of the Program's source code as you receive it, in any medium, provided that you conspicuously and appropriately publish on each copy an appropriate copyright notice; keep intact all notices stating that this License and any non-permissive terms added in accord with section 7 apply to the code; keep intact all notices of the absence of any warranty; and give all recipients a copy of this License along with the Program.

   You may charge any price or no price for each copy that you convey, and you may offer support or warranty protection for a fee.

5. Conveying Modified Source Versions.

   You may convey a work based on the Program, or the modifications to produce it from the Program, in the form of source code under the terms of section 4, provided that you also meet all of these conditions:

   a. The work must carry prominent notices stating that you modified it, and giving a relevant date.
   b. The work must carry prominent notices stating that it is released under this License and any conditions added under section 7. This requirement modifies the requirement in section 4 to "keep intact all notices".
   c. You must license the entire work, as a whole, under this License to anyone who comes into possession of a copy. This License will therefore apply, along with any applicable section 7 additional terms, to the whole of the work, and all its parts, regardless of how they are packaged. This License gives no permission to license the work in any other way, but it does not invalidate such permission if you have separately received it.
   d. If the work has interactive user interfaces, each must display Appropriate Legal Notices; however, if the Program has interactive interfaces that do not display Appropriate Legal Notices, your work need not make them do so.

   A compilation of a covered work with other separate and independent works, which are not by their nature extensions of the covered work, and which are not combined with it such as to form a larger program, in or on a volume of a storage or distribution medium, is called an "aggregate" if the compilation and its resulting copyright are not used to limit the access or legal rights of the compilation's users beyond what the individual works permit. Inclusion of a covered work in an aggregate does not cause this License to apply to the other parts of the aggregate.

6. Conveying Non-Source Forms.

   You may convey a covered work in object code form under the terms of sections 4 and 5, provided that you also convey the machine-readable Corresponding Source under the terms of this License, in one of these ways:

a. Convey the object code in, or embodied in, a physical product (including a physical distribution medium), accompanied by the Corresponding Source fixed on a durable physical medium customarily used for software interchange.
b. Convey the object code in, or embodied in, a physical product (including a physical distribution medium), accompanied by a written offer, valid for at least three years and valid for as long as you offer spare parts or customer support for that product model, to give anyone who possesses the object code either (1) a copy of the Corresponding Source for all the software in the product that is covered by this License, on a durable physical medium customarily used for software interchange, for a price no more than your reasonable cost of physically performing this conveying of source, or (2) access to copy the Corresponding Source from a network server at no charge.
c. Convey individual copies of the object code with a copy of the written offer to provide the Corresponding Source. This alternative is allowed only occasionally and noncommercially, and only if you received the object code with such an offer, in accord with subsection 6b.
d. Convey the object code by offering access from a designated place (gratis or for a charge), and offer equivalent access to the Corresponding Source in the same way through the same place at no further charge. You need not require recipients to copy the Corresponding Source along with the object code. If the place to copy the object code is a network server, the Corresponding Source may be on a different server (operated by you or a third party) that supports equivalent copying facilities, provided you maintain clear directions next to the object code saying where to find the Corresponding Source. Regardless of what server hosts the Corresponding Source, you remain obligated to ensure that it is available for as long as needed to satisfy these requirements.
e. Convey the object code using peer-to-peer transmission, provided you inform other peers where the object code and Corresponding Source of the work are being offered to the general public at no charge under subsection 6d.

A separable portion of the object code, whose source code is excluded from the Corresponding Source as a System Library, need not be included in conveying the object code work.

A "User Product" is either (1) a "consumer product", which means any tangible personal property which is normally used for personal, family, or household purposes, or (2) anything designed or sold for incorporation into a dwelling. In determining whether a product is a consumer product, doubtful cases shall be resolved in favor of coverage. For a particular product received by a particular user, "normally used" refers to a typical or common use of that class of product, regardless of the status of the particular user or of the way in which the particular user actually uses, or expects or is expected to use, the product. A product is a consumer product regardless of whether the product has substantial commercial, industrial or non-consumer uses, unless such uses represent the only significant mode of use of the product.

"Installation Information" for a User Product means any methods, procedures, authorization keys, or other information required to install and execute modified versions of a covered work in that User Product from a modified version of its Corresponding Source.

The information must suffice to ensure that the continued functioning of the modified object code is in no case prevented or interfered with solely because modification has been made.

If you convey an object code work under this section in, or with, or specifically for use in, a User Product, and the conveying occurs as part of a transaction in which the right of possession and use of the User Product is transferred to the recipient in perpetuity or for a fixed term (regardless of how the transaction is characterized), the Corresponding Source conveyed under this section must be accompanied by the Installation Information. But this requirement does not apply if neither you nor any third party retains the ability to install modified object code on the User Product (for example, the work has been installed in ROM).

The requirement to provide Installation Information does not include a requirement to continue to provide support service, warranty, or updates for a work that has been modified or installed by the recipient, or for the User Product in which it has been modified or installed. Access to a network may be denied when the modification itself materially and adversely affects the operation of the network or violates the rules and protocols for communication across the network.

Corresponding Source conveyed, and Installation Information provided, in accord with this section must be in a format that is publicly documented (and with an implementation available to the public in source code form), and must require no special password or key for unpacking, reading or copying.

7. Additional Terms.

   "Additional permissions" are terms that supplement the terms of this License by making exceptions from one or more of its conditions. Additional permissions that are applicable to the entire Program shall be treated as though they were included in this License, to the extent that they are valid under applicable law. If additional permissions apply only to part of the Program, that part may be used separately under those permissions, but the entire Program remains governed by this License without regard to the additional permissions.

   When you convey a copy of a covered work, you may at your option remove any additional permissions from that copy, or from any part of it. (Additional permissions may be written to require their own removal in certain cases when you modify the work.) You may place additional permissions on material, added by you to a covered work, for which you have or can give appropriate copyright permission.

   Notwithstanding any other provision of this License, for material you add to a covered work, you may (if authorized by the copyright holders of that material) supplement the terms of this License with terms:

   a. Disclaiming warranty or limiting liability differently from the terms of sections 15 and 16 of this License; or
   b. Requiring preservation of specified reasonable legal notices or author attributions in that material or in the Appropriate Legal Notices displayed by works containing it; or
   c. Prohibiting misrepresentation of the origin of that material, or requiring that modified versions of such material be marked in reasonable ways as different from the original version; or

d. Limiting the use for publicity purposes of names of licensors or authors of the material; or
e. Declining to grant rights under trademark law for use of some trade names, trademarks, or service marks; or
f. Requiring indemnification of licensors and authors of that material by anyone who conveys the material (or modified versions of it) with contractual assumptions of liability to the recipient, for any liability that these contractual assumptions directly impose on those licensors and authors.

All other non-permissive additional terms are considered "further restrictions" within the meaning of section 10. If the Program as you received it, or any part of it, contains a notice stating that it is governed by this License along with a term that is a further restriction, you may remove that term. If a license document contains a further restriction but permits relicensing or conveying under this License, you may add to a covered work material governed by the terms of that license document, provided that the further restriction does not survive such relicensing or conveying.

If you add terms to a covered work in accord with this section, you must place, in the relevant source files, a statement of the additional terms that apply to those files, or a notice indicating where to find the applicable terms.

Additional terms, permissive or non-permissive, may be stated in the form of a separately written license, or stated as exceptions; the above requirements apply either way.

8. Termination.

You may not propagate or modify a covered work except as expressly provided under this License. Any attempt otherwise to propagate or modify it is void, and will automatically terminate your rights under this License (including any patent licenses granted under the third paragraph of section 11).

However, if you cease all violation of this License, then your license from a particular copyright holder is reinstated (a) provisionally, unless and until the copyright holder explicitly and finally terminates your license, and (b) permanently, if the copyright holder fails to notify you of the violation by some reasonable means prior to 60 days after the cessation.

Moreover, your license from a particular copyright holder is reinstated permanently if the copyright holder notifies you of the violation by some reasonable means, this is the first time you have received notice of violation of this License (for any work) from that copyright holder, and you cure the violation prior to 30 days after your receipt of the notice.

Termination of your rights under this section does not terminate the licenses of parties who have received copies or rights from you under this License. If your rights have been terminated and not permanently reinstated, you do not qualify to receive new licenses for the same material under section 10.

9. Acceptance Not Required for Having Copies.

You are not required to accept this License in order to receive or run a copy of the Program. Ancillary propagation of a covered work occurring solely as a consequence of using peer-to-peer transmission to receive a copy likewise does not require acceptance.

However, nothing other than this License grants you permission to propagate or modify any covered work. These actions infringe copyright if you do not accept this License. Therefore, by modifying or propagating a covered work, you indicate your acceptance of this License to do so.

10. Automatic Licensing of Downstream Recipients.

    Each time you convey a covered work, the recipient automatically receives a license from the original licensors, to run, modify and propagate that work, subject to this License. You are not responsible for enforcing compliance by third parties with this License.

    An "entity transaction" is a transaction transferring control of an organization, or substantially all assets of one, or subdividing an organization, or merging organizations. If propagation of a covered work results from an entity transaction, each party to that transaction who receives a copy of the work also receives whatever licenses to the work the party's predecessor in interest had or could give under the previous paragraph, plus a right to possession of the Corresponding Source of the work from the predecessor in interest, if the predecessor has it or can get it with reasonable efforts.

    You may not impose any further restrictions on the exercise of the rights granted or affirmed under this License. For example, you may not impose a license fee, royalty, or other charge for exercise of rights granted under this License, and you may not initiate litigation (including a cross-claim or counterclaim in a lawsuit) alleging that any patent claim is infringed by making, using, selling, offering for sale, or importing the Program or any portion of it.

11. Patents.

    A "contributor" is a copyright holder who authorizes use under this License of the Program or a work on which the Program is based. The work thus licensed is called the contributor's "contributor version".

    A contributor's "essential patent claims" are all patent claims owned or controlled by the contributor, whether already acquired or hereafter acquired, that would be infringed by some manner, permitted by this License, of making, using, or selling its contributor version, but do not include claims that would be infringed only as a consequence of further modification of the contributor version. For purposes of this definition, "control" includes the right to grant patent sublicenses in a manner consistent with the requirements of this License.

    Each contributor grants you a non-exclusive, worldwide, royalty-free patent license under the contributor's essential patent claims, to make, use, sell, offer for sale, import and otherwise run, modify and propagate the contents of its contributor version.

    In the following three paragraphs, a "patent license" is any express agreement or commitment, however denominated, not to enforce a patent (such as an express permission to practice a patent or covenant not to sue for patent infringement). To "grant" such a patent license to a party means to make such an agreement or commitment not to enforce a patent against the party.

    If you convey a covered work, knowingly relying on a patent license, and the Corresponding Source of the work is not available for anyone to copy, free of charge and under the terms of this License, through a publicly available network server or other readily accessible means, then you must either (1) cause the Corresponding Source to be so available, or (2) arrange to deprive yourself of the benefit of the patent license for this particular work, or (3) arrange, in a manner consistent with the requirements of this License, to extend the patent license to downstream recipients. “Knowingly relying” means you have actual knowledge that, but for the patent license, your conveying the covered work in a country, or your recipient’s use of the covered work in a country, would infringe one or more identifiable patents in that country that you have reason to believe are valid.

If, pursuant to or in connection with a single transaction or arrangement, you convey, or propagate by procuring conveyance of, a covered work, and grant a patent license to some of the parties receiving the covered work authorizing them to use, propagate, modify or convey a specific copy of the covered work, then the patent license you grant is automatically extended to all recipients of the covered work and works based on it.

A patent license is “discriminatory” if it does not include within the scope of its coverage, prohibits the exercise of, or is conditioned on the non-exercise of one or more of the rights that are specifically granted under this License. You may not convey a covered work if you are a party to an arrangement with a third party that is in the business of distributing software, under which you make payment to the third party based on the extent of your activity of conveying the work, and under which the third party grants, to any of the parties who would receive the covered work from you, a discriminatory patent license (a) in connection with copies of the covered work conveyed by you (or copies made from those copies), or (b) primarily for and in connection with specific products or compilations that contain the covered work, unless you entered into that arrangement, or that patent license was granted, prior to 28 March 2007.

Nothing in this License shall be construed as excluding or limiting any implied license or other defenses to infringement that may otherwise be available to you under applicable patent law.

12. No Surrender of Others’ Freedom.

    If conditions are imposed on you (whether by court order, agreement or otherwise) that contradict the conditions of this License, they do not excuse you from the conditions of this License. If you cannot convey a covered work so as to satisfy simultaneously your obligations under this License and any other pertinent obligations, then as a consequence you may not convey it at all. For example, if you agree to terms that obligate you to collect a royalty for further conveying from those to whom you convey the Program, the only way you could satisfy both those terms and this License would be to refrain entirely from conveying the Program.

13. Use with the GNU Affero General Public License.

    Notwithstanding any other provision of this License, you have permission to link or combine any covered work with a work licensed under version 3 of the GNU Affero General Public License into a single combined work, and to convey the resulting work. The terms of this License will continue to apply to the part which is the covered work, but the special requirements of the GNU Affero General Public License, section 13, concerning interaction through a network will apply to the combination as such.

14. Revised Versions of this License.

The Free Software Foundation may publish revised and/or new versions of the GNU General Public License from time to time. Such new versions will be similar in spirit to the present version, but may differ in detail to address new problems or concerns.

Each version is given a distinguishing version number. If the Program specifies that a certain numbered version of the GNU General Public License "or any later version" applies to it, you have the option of following the terms and conditions either of that numbered version or of any later version published by the Free Software Foundation. If the Program does not specify a version number of the GNU General Public License, you may choose any version ever published by the Free Software Foundation.

If the Program specifies that a proxy can decide which future versions of the GNU General Public License can be used, that proxy's public statement of acceptance of a version permanently authorizes you to choose that version for the Program.

Later license versions may give you additional or different permissions. However, no additional obligations are imposed on any author or copyright holder as a result of your choosing to follow a later version.

15. Disclaimer of Warranty.

    THERE IS NO WARRANTY FOR THE PROGRAM, TO THE EXTENT PERMITTED BY APPLICABLE LAW. EXCEPT WHEN OTHERWISE STATED IN WRITING THE COPYRIGHT HOLDERS AND/OR OTHER PARTIES PROVIDE THE PROGRAM "AS IS" WITHOUT WARRANTY OF ANY KIND, EITHER EXPRESSED OR IMPLIED, INCLUDING, BUT NOT LIMITED TO, THE IMPLIED WARRANTIES OF MERCHANTABILITY AND FITNESS FOR A PARTICULAR PURPOSE. THE ENTIRE RISK AS TO THE QUALITY AND PERFORMANCE OF THE PROGRAM IS WITH YOU. SHOULD THE PROGRAM PROVE DEFECTIVE, YOU ASSUME THE COST OF ALL NECESSARY SERVICING, REPAIR OR CORRECTION.

16. Limitation of Liability.

    IN NO EVENT UNLESS REQUIRED BY APPLICABLE LAW OR AGREED TO IN WRITING WILL ANY COPYRIGHT HOLDER, OR ANY OTHER PARTY WHO MODIFIES AND/OR CONVEYS THE PROGRAM AS PERMITTED ABOVE, BE LIABLE TO YOU FOR DAMAGES, INCLUDING ANY GENERAL, SPECIAL, INCIDENTAL OR CONSEQUENTIAL DAMAGES ARISING OUT OF THE USE OR INABILITY TO USE THE PROGRAM (INCLUDING BUT NOT LIMITED TO LOSS OF DATA OR DATA BEING RENDERED INACCURATE OR LOSSES SUSTAINED BY YOU OR THIRD PARTIES OR A FAILURE OF THE PROGRAM TO OPERATE WITH ANY OTHER PROGRAMS), EVEN IF SUCH HOLDER OR OTHER PARTY HAS BEEN ADVISED OF THE POSSIBILITY OF SUCH DAMAGES.

17. Interpretation of Sections 15 and 16.

    If the disclaimer of warranty and limitation of liability provided above cannot be given local legal effect according to their terms, reviewing courts shall apply local law that most closely approximates an absolute waiver of all civil liability in connection with the Program, unless a warranty or assumption of liability accompanies a copy of the Program in return for a fee.

END OF TERMS AND CONDITIONS

How to Apply These Terms to Your New Programs

If you develop a new program, and you want it to be of the greatest possible use to the public, the best way to achieve this is to make it free software which everyone can redistribute and change under these terms.

To do so, attach the following notices to the program. It is safest to attach them to the start of each source file to most effectively state the exclusion of warranty; and each file should have at least the "copyright" line and a pointer to where the full notice is found.

```
one line to give the program's name and a brief idea of what it does.
Copyright (C) year name of author

This program is free software: you can redistribute it and/or modify
it under the terms of the GNU General Public License as published by
the Free Software Foundation, either version 3 of the License, or (at
your option) any later version.

This program is distributed in the hope that it will be useful, but
WITHOUT ANY WARRANTY; without even the implied warranty of
MERCHANTABILITY or FITNESS FOR A PARTICULAR PURPOSE.  See the GNU
General Public License for more details.

You should have received a copy of the GNU General Public License
along with this program.  If not, see http://www.gnu.org/licenses/.
```

Also add information on how to contact you by electronic and paper mail.

If the program does terminal interaction, make it output a short notice like this when it starts in an interactive mode:

```
program Copyright (C) year name of author
This program comes with ABSOLUTELY NO WARRANTY; for details type 'show w'.
This is free software, and you are welcome to redistribute it
under certain conditions; type 'show c' for details.
```

The hypothetical commands '`show w`' and '`show c`' should show the appropriate parts of the General Public License. Of course, your program's commands might be different; for a GUI interface, you would use an "about box".

You should also get your employer (if you work as a programmer) or school, if any, to sign a "copyright disclaimer" for the program, if necessary. For more information on this, and how to apply and follow the GNU GPL, see `http://www.gnu.org/licenses/`.

The GNU General Public License does not permit incorporating your program into proprietary programs. If your program is a subroutine library, you may consider it more useful to permit linking proprietary applications with the library. If this is what you want to do, use the GNU Lesser General Public License instead of this License. But first, please read `http://www.gnu.org/philosophy/why-not-lgpl.html`.

GNU Free Documentation License

Version 1.3, 3 November 2008

0. PREAMBLE

The purpose of this License is to make a manual, textbook, or other functional and useful document *free* in the sense of freedom: to assure everyone the effective freedom to copy and redistribute it, with or without modifying it, either commercially or noncommercially. Secondarily, this License preserves for the author and publisher a way to get credit for their work, while not being considered responsible for modifications made by others.

This License is a kind of "copyleft", which means that derivative works of the document must themselves be free in the same sense. It complements the GNU General Public License, which is a copyleft license designed for free software.

We have designed this License in order to use it for manuals for free software, because free software needs free documentation: a free program should come with manuals providing the same freedoms that the software does. But this License is not limited to software manuals; it can be used for any textual work, regardless of subject matter or whether it is published as a printed book. We recommend this License principally for works whose purpose is instruction or reference.

1. APPLICABILITY AND DEFINITIONS

This License applies to any manual or other work, in any medium, that contains a notice placed by the copyright holder saying it can be distributed under the terms of this License. Such a notice grants a world-wide, royalty-free license, unlimited in duration, to use that work under the conditions stated herein. The "Document", below, refers to any such manual or work. Any member of the public is a licensee, and is addressed as "you". You accept the license if you copy, modify or distribute the work in a way requiring permission under copyright law.

A "Modified Version" of the Document means any work containing the Document or a portion of it, either copied verbatim, or with modifications and/or translated into another language.

A "Secondary Section" is a named appendix or a front-matter section of the Document that deals exclusively with the relationship of the publishers or authors of the Document to the Document's overall subject (or to related matters) and contains nothing that could fall directly within that overall subject. (Thus, if the Document is in part a textbook of mathematics, a Secondary Section may not explain any mathematics.) The relationship could be a matter of historical connection with the subject or with related matters, or of legal, commercial, philosophical, ethical or political position regarding them.

The "Invariant Sections" are certain Secondary Sections whose titles are designated, as being those of Invariant Sections, in the notice that says that the Document is released under this License. If a section does not fit the above definition of Secondary then it is not allowed to be designated as Invariant. The Document may contain zero Invariant Sections. If the Document does not identify any Invariant Sections then there are none.

The "Cover Texts" are certain short passages of text that are listed, as Front-Cover Texts or Back-Cover Texts, in the notice that says that the Document is released under this License. A Front-Cover Text may be at most 5 words, and a Back-Cover Text may be at most 25 words.

A "Transparent" copy of the Document means a machine-readable copy, represented in a format whose specification is available to the general public, that is suitable for revising the document straightforwardly with generic text editors or (for images composed of pixels) generic paint programs or (for drawings) some widely available drawing editor, and that is suitable for input to text formatters or for automatic translation to a variety of formats suitable for input to text formatters. A copy made in an otherwise Transparent file format whose markup, or absence of markup, has been arranged to thwart or discourage subsequent modification by readers is not Transparent. An image format is not Transparent if used for any substantial amount of text. A copy that is not "Transparent" is called "Opaque".

Examples of suitable formats for Transparent copies include plain ASCII without markup, Texinfo input format, LaTeX input format, SGML or XML using a publicly available DTD, and standard-conforming simple HTML, PostScript or PDF designed for human modification. Examples of transparent image formats include PNG, XCF and JPG. Opaque formats include proprietary formats that can be read and edited only by proprietary word processors, SGML or XML for which the DTD and/or processing tools are not generally available, and the machine-generated HTML, PostScript or PDF produced by some word processors for output purposes only.

The "Title Page" means, for a printed book, the title page itself, plus such following pages as are needed to hold, legibly, the material this License requires to appear in the title page. For works in formats which do not have any title page as such, "Title Page" means the text near the most prominent appearance of the work's title, preceding the beginning of the body of the text.

The "publisher" means any person or entity that distributes copies of the Document to the public.

A section "Entitled XYZ" means a named subunit of the Document whose title either is precisely XYZ or contains XYZ in parentheses following text that translates XYZ in another language. (Here XYZ stands for a specific section name mentioned below, such as "Acknowledgements", "Dedications", "Endorsements", or "History".) To "Preserve the Title" of such a section when you modify the Document means that it remains a section "Entitled XYZ" according to this definition.

The Document may include Warranty Disclaimers next to the notice which states that this License applies to the Document. These Warranty Disclaimers are considered to be included by reference in this License, but only as regards disclaiming warranties: any other implication that these Warranty Disclaimers may have is void and has no effect on the meaning of this License.

2. VERBATIM COPYING

You may copy and distribute the Document in any medium, either commercially or noncommercially, provided that this License, the copyright notices, and the license notice saying this License applies to the Document are reproduced in all copies, and that you add no other conditions whatsoever to those of this License. You may not use technical measures to obstruct or control the reading or further copying of the copies you make or distribute. However, you may accept compensation in exchange for copies. If you distribute a large enough number of copies you must also follow the conditions in section 3.

You may also lend copies, under the same conditions stated above, and you may publicly display copies.

3. COPYING IN QUANTITY

If you publish printed copies (or copies in media that commonly have printed covers) of the Document, numbering more than 100, and the Document's license notice requires Cover Texts, you must enclose the copies in covers that carry, clearly and legibly, all these Cover Texts: Front-Cover Texts on the front cover, and Back-Cover Texts on the back cover. Both covers must also clearly and legibly identify you as the publisher of these copies. The front cover must present the full title with all words of the title equally prominent and visible. You may add other material on the covers in addition. Copying with changes limited to the covers, as long as they preserve the title of the Document and satisfy these conditions, can be treated as verbatim copying in other respects.

If the required texts for either cover are too voluminous to fit legibly, you should put the first ones listed (as many as fit reasonably) on the actual cover, and continue the rest onto adjacent pages.

If you publish or distribute Opaque copies of the Document numbering more than 100, you must either include a machine-readable Transparent copy along with each Opaque copy, or state in or with each Opaque copy a computer-network location from which the general network-using public has access to download using public-standard network protocols a complete Transparent copy of the Document, free of added material. If you use the latter option, you must take reasonably prudent steps, when you begin distribution of Opaque copies in quantity, to ensure that this Transparent copy will remain thus accessible at the stated location until at least one year after the last time you distribute an Opaque copy (directly or through your agents or retailers) of that edition to the public.

It is requested, but not required, that you contact the authors of the Document well before redistributing any large number of copies, to give them a chance to provide you with an updated version of the Document.

4. MODIFICATIONS

You may copy and distribute a Modified Version of the Document under the conditions of sections 2 and 3 above, provided that you release the Modified Version under precisely this License, with the Modified Version filling the role of the Document, thus licensing distribution and modification of the Modified Version to whoever possesses a copy of it. In addition, you must do these things in the Modified Version:

A. Use in the Title Page (and on the covers, if any) a title distinct from that of the Document, and from those of previous versions (which should, if there were any, be listed in the History section of the Document). You may use the same title as a previous version if the original publisher of that version gives permission.

B. List on the Title Page, as authors, one or more persons or entities responsible for authorship of the modifications in the Modified Version, together with at least five of the principal authors of the Document (all of its principal authors, if it has fewer than five), unless they release you from this requirement.

C. State on the Title page the name of the publisher of the Modified Version, as the publisher.

D. Preserve all the copyright notices of the Document.

E. Add an appropriate copyright notice for your modifications adjacent to the other copyright notices.

F. Include, immediately after the copyright notices, a license notice giving the public permission to use the Modified Version under the terms of this License, in the form shown in the Addendum below.

G. Preserve in that license notice the full lists of Invariant Sections and required Cover Texts given in the Document's license notice.

H. Include an unaltered copy of this License.

I. Preserve the section Entitled "History", Preserve its Title, and add to it an item stating at least the title, year, new authors, and publisher of the Modified Version as given on the Title Page. If there is no section Entitled "History" in the Document, create one stating the title, year, authors, and publisher of the Document as given on its Title Page, then add an item describing the Modified Version as stated in the previous sentence.

J. Preserve the network location, if any, given in the Document for public access to a Transparent copy of the Document, and likewise the network locations given in the Document for previous versions it was based on. These may be placed in the "History" section. You may omit a network location for a work that was published at least four years before the Document itself, or if the original publisher of the version it refers to gives permission.

K. For any section Entitled "Acknowledgements" or "Dedications", Preserve the Title of the section, and preserve in the section all the substance and tone of each of the contributor acknowledgements and/or dedications given therein.

L. Preserve all the Invariant Sections of the Document, unaltered in their text and in their titles. Section numbers or the equivalent are not considered part of the section titles.

M. Delete any section Entitled "Endorsements". Such a section may not be included in the Modified Version.

N. Do not retitle any existing section to be Entitled "Endorsements" or to conflict in title with any Invariant Section.

O. Preserve any Warranty Disclaimers.

If the Modified Version includes new front-matter sections or appendices that qualify as Secondary Sections and contain no material copied from the Document, you may at your option designate some or all of these sections as invariant. To do this, add their titles to the list of Invariant Sections in the Modified Version's license notice. These titles must be distinct from any other section titles.

You may add a section Entitled "Endorsements", provided it contains nothing but endorsements of your Modified Version by various parties—for example, statements of peer review or that the text has been approved by an organization as the authoritative definition of a standard.

You may add a passage of up to five words as a Front-Cover Text, and a passage of up to 25 words as a Back-Cover Text, to the end of the list of Cover Texts in the Modified Version. Only one passage of Front-Cover Text and one of Back-Cover Text may be added by (or through arrangements made by) any one entity. If the Document already includes a cover text for the same cover, previously added by you or by arrangement made by the same entity you are acting on behalf of, you may not add another; but you may replace the old one, on explicit permission from the previous publisher that added the old one.

The author(s) and publisher(s) of the Document do not by this License give permission to use their names for publicity for or to assert or imply endorsement of any Modified Version.

5. COMBINING DOCUMENTS

   You may combine the Document with other documents released under this License, under the terms defined in section 4 above for modified versions, provided that you include in the combination all of the Invariant Sections of all of the original documents, unmodified, and list them all as Invariant Sections of your combined work in its license notice, and that you preserve all their Warranty Disclaimers.

   The combined work need only contain one copy of this License, and multiple identical Invariant Sections may be replaced with a single copy. If there are multiple Invariant Sections with the same name but different contents, make the title of each such section unique by adding at the end of it, in parentheses, the name of the original author or publisher of that section if known, or else a unique number. Make the same adjustment to the section titles in the list of Invariant Sections in the license notice of the combined work.

   In the combination, you must combine any sections Entitled "History" in the various original documents, forming one section Entitled "History"; likewise combine any sections Entitled "Acknowledgements", and any sections Entitled "Dedications". You must delete all sections Entitled "Endorsements."

6. COLLECTIONS OF DOCUMENTS

   You may make a collection consisting of the Document and other documents released under this License, and replace the individual copies of this License in the various documents with a single copy that is included in the collection, provided that you follow the rules of this License for verbatim copying of each of the documents in all other respects.

   You may extract a single document from such a collection, and distribute it individually under this License, provided you insert a copy of this License into the extracted document, and follow this License in all other respects regarding verbatim copying of that document.

7. AGGREGATION WITH INDEPENDENT WORKS

   A compilation of the Document or its derivatives with other separate and independent documents or works, in or on a volume of a storage or distribution medium, is called an "aggregate" if the copyright resulting from the compilation is not used to limit the legal rights of the compilation's users beyond what the individual works permit. When the Document is included in an aggregate, this License does not apply to the other works in the aggregate which are not themselves derivative works of the Document.

   If the Cover Text requirement of section 3 is applicable to these copies of the Document, then if the Document is less than one half of the entire aggregate, the Document's Cover Texts may be placed on covers that bracket the Document within the aggregate, or the electronic equivalent of covers if the Document is in electronic form. Otherwise they must appear on printed covers that bracket the whole aggregate.

8. TRANSLATION

   Translation is considered a kind of modification, so you may distribute translations of the Document under the terms of section 4. Replacing Invariant Sections with translations requires special permission from their copyright holders, but you may include translations of some or all Invariant Sections in addition to the original versions of these Invariant Sections. You may include a translation of this License, and all the license notices in the Document, and any Warranty Disclaimers, provided that you also include the original English version of this License and the original versions of those notices and disclaimers. In case of a disagreement between the translation and the original version of this License or a notice or disclaimer, the original version will prevail.

   If a section in the Document is Entitled "Acknowledgements", "Dedications", or "History", the requirement (section 4) to Preserve its Title (section 1) will typically require changing the actual title.

9. TERMINATION

   You may not copy, modify, sublicense, or distribute the Document except as expressly provided under this License. Any attempt otherwise to copy, modify, sublicense, or distribute it is void, and will automatically terminate your rights under this License.

   However, if you cease all violation of this License, then your license from a particular copyright holder is reinstated (a) provisionally, unless and until the copyright holder explicitly and finally terminates your license, and (b) permanently, if the copyright holder fails to notify you of the violation by some reasonable means prior to 60 days after the cessation.

   Moreover, your license from a particular copyright holder is reinstated permanently if the copyright holder notifies you of the violation by some reasonable means, this is the first time you have received notice of violation of this License (for any work) from that copyright holder, and you cure the violation prior to 30 days after your receipt of the notice.

   Termination of your rights under this section does not terminate the licenses of parties who have received copies or rights from you under this License. If your rights have been terminated and not permanently reinstated, receipt of a copy of some or all of the same material does not give you any rights to use it.

10. FUTURE REVISIONS OF THIS LICENSE

    The Free Software Foundation may publish new, revised versions of the GNU Free Documentation License from time to time. Such new versions will be similar in spirit to the present version, but may differ in detail to address new problems or concerns. See `http://www.gnu.org/copyleft/`.

    Each version of the License is given a distinguishing version number. If the Document specifies that a particular numbered version of this License "or any later version" applies to it, you have the option of following the terms and conditions either of that specified version or of any later version that has been published (not as a draft) by the Free Software Foundation. If the Document does not specify a version number of this License, you may choose any version ever published (not as a draft) by the Free Software Foundation. If the Document specifies that a proxy can decide which future versions of this License can be used, that proxy's public statement of acceptance of a version permanently authorizes you to choose that version for the Document.

11. RELICENSING

    "Massive Multiauthor Collaboration Site" (or "MMC Site") means any World Wide Web server that publishes copyrightable works and also provides prominent facilities for anybody to edit those works. A public wiki that anybody can edit is an example of such a server. A "Massive Multiauthor Collaboration" (or "MMC") contained in the site means any set of copyrightable works thus published on the MMC site.

    "CC-BY-SA" means the Creative Commons Attribution-Share Alike 3.0 license published by Creative Commons Corporation, a not-for-profit corporation with a principal place of business in San Francisco, California, as well as future copyleft versions of that license published by that same organization.

    "Incorporate" means to publish or republish a Document, in whole or in part, as part of another Document.

    An MMC is "eligible for relicensing" if it is licensed under this License, and if all works that were first published under this License somewhere other than this MMC, and subsequently incorporated in whole or in part into the MMC, (1) had no cover texts or invariant sections, and (2) were thus incorporated prior to November 1, 2008.

    The operator of an MMC Site may republish an MMC contained in the site under CC-BY-SA on the same site at any time before August 1, 2009, provided the MMC is eligible for relicensing.

ADDENDUM: How to use this License for your documents

To use this License in a document you have written, include a copy of the License in the document and put the following copyright and license notices just after the title page:

```
Copyright (C)  year  your name.
Permission is granted to copy, distribute and/or modify this document
under the terms of the GNU Free Documentation License, Version 1.3
or any later version published by the Free Software Foundation;
with no Invariant Sections, no Front-Cover Texts, and no Back-Cover
Texts.  A copy of the license is included in the section entitled ``GNU
Free Documentation License''.
```

If you have Invariant Sections, Front-Cover Texts and Back-Cover Texts, replace the "with...Texts." line with this:

```
with the Invariant Sections being list their titles, with
the Front-Cover Texts being list, and with the Back-Cover Texts
being list.
```

If you have Invariant Sections without Cover Texts, or some other combination of the three, merge those two alternatives to suit the situation.

If your document contains nontrivial examples of program code, we recommend releasing these examples in parallel under your choice of free software license, such as the GNU General Public License, to permit their use in free software.

Funding Free Software

If you want to have more free software a few years from now, it makes sense for you to help encourage people to contribute funds for its development. The most effective approach known is to encourage commercial redistributors to donate.

Users of free software systems can boost the pace of development by encouraging for-a-fee distributors to donate part of their selling price to free software developers—the Free Software Foundation, and others.

The way to convince distributors to do this is to demand it and expect it from them. So when you compare distributors, judge them partly by how much they give to free software development. Show distributors they must compete to be the one who gives the most.

To make this approach work, you must insist on numbers that you can compare, such as, "We will donate ten dollars to the Frobnitz project for each disk sold." Don't be satisfied with a vague promise, such as "A portion of the profits are donated," since it doesn't give a basis for comparison.

Even a precise fraction "of the profits from this disk" is not very meaningful, since creative accounting and unrelated business decisions can greatly alter what fraction of the sales price counts as profit. If the price you pay is $50, ten percent of the profit is probably less than a dollar; it might be a few cents, or nothing at all.

Some redistributors do development work themselves. This is useful too; but to keep everyone honest, you need to inquire how much they do, and what kind. Some kinds of development make much more long-term difference than others. For example, maintaining a separate version of a program contributes very little; maintaining the standard version of a program for the whole community contributes much. Easy new ports contribute little, since someone else would surely do them; difficult ports such as adding a new CPU to the GNU Compiler Collection contribute more; major new features or packages contribute the most.

By establishing the idea that supporting further development is "the proper thing to do" when distributing free software for a fee, we can assure a steady flow of resources into making more free software.

Library Index

E

Environment Variable 19, 20, 21, 22, 23, 24

F

FDL, GNU Free Documentation License 67

I

Implementation specific setting 20, 22, 23, 24
Introduction 1

www.ingramcontent.com/pod-product-compliance
Lightning Source LLC
Chambersburg PA
CBHW060456060326
40689CB00020B/4553
9789888406975